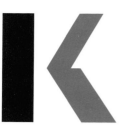

Kaplan Publishing are constantly finding new ways to make a difference to your studies and our exciting online resources really do offer something different to students looking for exam success.

KU-265-750

This book comes with free MyKaplan online resources so that you can study anytime, anywhere. **This free online resource is not sold separately and is included in the price of the book.**

Having purchased this book, you have access to the following online study materials:

CONTENT	AAT	
	Text	Kit
Electronic version of the book	✓	✓
Progress tests with instant answers	✓	
Mock assessments online	✓	✓
Material updates	✓	✓

How to access your online resources

Kaplan Financial students will already have a MyKaplan account and these extra resources will be available to you online. You do not need to register again, as this process was completed when you enrolled. If you are having problems accessing online materials, please ask your course administrator.

If you are not studying with Kaplan and did not purchase your book via a Kaplan website, to unlock your extra online resources please go to www.mykaplan.co.uk/addabook (even if you have set up an account and registered books previously). You will then need to enter the ISBN number (on the title page and back cover) and the unique pass key number contained in the scratch panel below to gain access. You will also be required to enter additional information during this process to set up or confirm your account details.

If you purchased through Kaplan Flexible Learning or via the Kaplan Publishing website you will automatically receive an e-mail invitation to MyKaplan. Please register your details using this email to gain access to your content. If you do not receive the e-mail or book content, please contact Kaplan Publishing.

Your Code and Information

This code can only be used once for the registration of one book online. This registration and your online content will expire when the final sittings for the examinations covered by this book have taken place. Please allow one hour from the time you submit your book details for us to process your request.

Please scratch the film to access your MyKaplan code.

Please be aware that this code is case-sensitive and you will need to include the dashes within the passcode, but not when entering the ISBN. For further technical support, please visit www.MyKaplan.co.uk

LS

XT

work

2016

This Study Text supports study for the following AAT qualifications:

AAT Foundation Certificate in Accounting – Level 2

AAT Foundation Diploma in Accounting and Business – Level 2

AAT Foundation Certificate in Bookkeeping – Level 2

AAT Foundation Award in Accounting Software – Level 2

AAT Level 2 Award in Accounting Skills to Run Your Business

AAT Foundation Certificate in Accounting at SCQF Level 5

British Library Cataloguing-in-Publication Data

A catalogue record for this book is available from the British Library.

Published by
Kaplan Publishing UK
Unit 2, The Business Centre
Molly Millars Lane
Wokingham
Berkshire
RG41 2QZ

ISBN: 978-1-78740-260-7

The text in this material and any others made available by any Kaplan Group company does not amount to advice on a particular matter and should not be taken as such. No reliance should be placed on the content as the basis for any investment or other decision or in connection with any advice given to third parties. Please consult your appropriate professional adviser as necessary. Kaplan Publishing Limited and all other Kaplan group companies expressly disclaim all liability to any person in respect of any losses or other claims, whether direct, indirect, incidental, consequential or otherwise arising in relation to the use of such materials.

© Kaplan Financial Limited, 2018

Printed and bound in Great Britain.

CONTENTS

KAPLAN PUBLISHING

INTRODUCTION

HOW TO USE THESE MATERIALS

These Kaplan Publishing learning materials have been carefully designed to make your learning experience as easy as possible and to give you the best chance of success in your AAT assessments.

They contain a number of features to help you in the study process.

The sections on the Unit Guide, the Assessment and Study Skills should be read before you commence your studies.

They are designed to familiarise you with the nature and content of the assessment and to give you tips on how best to approach your studies.

STUDY TEXT

This study text has been specially prepared for the revised AAT qualification introduced in September 2016

It is written in a practical and interactive style:

- key terms and concepts are clearly defined

- all topics are illustrated with practical examples with clearly worked solutions based on sample tasks provided by the AAT in the new examining style

- frequent activities throughout the chapters ensure that what you have learnt is regularly reinforced

- 'pitfalls' and 'examination tips' help you avoid commonly made mistakes and help you focus on what is required to perform well in your examination

- 'Test your understanding' activities are included within each chapter to apply your learning and develop your understanding.

ICONS

The chapters include the following icons throughout.

They are designed to assist you in your studies by identifying key definitions and the points at which you can test yourself on the knowledge gained.

 Definition

These sections explain important areas of Knowledge which must be understood and reproduced in an assessment.

 Example

The illustrative examples can be used to help develop an understanding of topics before attempting the activity exercises.

 Test your understanding

These are exercises which give the opportunity to assess your understanding of all the assessment areas.

Quality and accuracy are of the utmost importance to us so if you spot an error in any of our products, please send an email to mykaplanreporting@kaplan.com with full details, or follow the link to the feedback form in MyKaplan.

Our Quality Co-ordinator will work with our technical team to verify the error and take action to ensure it is corrected in future editions.

UNIT GUIDE

Introduction

This unit is about control accounts, journals and methods of payment. It takes students through reconciliation processes and the use of the journal to the stage of re-drafting the trial balance, following initial adjustments.

This unit covers more complex Foundation Diploma bookkeeping procedures, which will enable students to develop their understanding of the relationship between the various accounting records, and consolidate their knowledge of double-entry bookkeeping. Students will gain the confidence they need to perform well in the workplace and the unit will prepare them for greater responsibility.

Students will develop the ability to prepare the value added tax (VAT) control account as well as the sales and purchases ledger control accounts, including reconciliation with the sales and purchases ledgers. They will use the journal to record a variety of transactions, including the correction of errors. Students will be able to redraft the initial trial balance, following adjustments, and be able to identify different methods of payment and their use. They will learn to update the cash book following receipt of a bank statement, and also how to prepare a bank reconciliation statement.

This unit builds on the knowledge and skills acquired from studying Bookkeeping Transactions. Studying Bookkeeping Controls and consolidating the double-entry bookkeeping skills gained in Bookkeeping Transactions will also provide an important foundation for the financial accounting units at Advanced Diploma in Accounting – Advanced Bookkeeping and Final Accounts Preparation.

Bookkeeping Controls is a mandatory unit in this qualification.

Learning objectives

On completion of these units the learner will be able to:

- reconcile a bank statement with the cash book

- understand the use of the journal

- open a new set of double entry bookkeeping records using the journal

- use the journal to correct errors disclosed and not disclosed by the trial balance

- create and clear a suspense account using the journal

- use the journal to record other transactions, such as irrecoverable debts, contras and payroll entries

- understand key payment methods and the clearing system

- understand the importance of document retention

- understand and reconcile control accounts

- prepare sales and purchase ledger and VAT control accounts

- reconcile sales and purchase ledger control accounts.

Scope of content

The specific items contained within each learning outcome and where to find them in this study text are detailed below.

Chapter

1   Understand payment methods

1.1   Identify the appropriate use of different payment methods

8

Students need to know:

- different payment methods: cash, cheque, debit card, credit card, bank draft, standing order, direct debit, BACS (Bankers' Automated Clearing Services) direct credit, CHAPS (Clearing House Automated Payment System), Faster Payments.

1.2 Identify the effect of different payment methods on the bank balance

8

Students need to know:

- that different payment methods affect the bank balance in different ways: reduce funds on date of payment, reduce funds at later date, no effect.

2 Understand controls in a bookkeeping system

2.1 Identify the purpose of control accounts

Students need to know:

- the purpose of the sales and purchases ledger control accounts (part of the double-entry bookkeeping system)

5

- the purpose of the VAT control account.

5

2.2 Identify the purpose of reconciliation

Students need to know:

- reasons for reconciling the sales and purchases ledger control accounts with the sales and purchases ledgers

5

- reasons for reconciling the bank statement with the cash book.

7

2.3 Identify the purpose of the journal

Students need to know:

- the purpose of the journal as a book of prime entry

4

- transactions that are recorded in the journal: opening entries for a new business, irrecoverable debts written off, payroll transactions

4, 6

- errors that are corrected through the journal and the effect on the trial balance: disclosed and not disclosed

4

- names of errors not disclosed by trial balance: commission, omission, original entry, principle, reversal of entries, compensating errors.

4

3 Use control accounts

3.1 Produce control accounts

Students need to be able to:

- prepare control accounts, sales ledger, purchases ledger, VAT — 5

- total and balance control accounts: balance carried down, balance brought down. — 5

3.2 Reconcile control accounts

Students need to be able to:

- total the balances of the individual sales and purchases ledger accounts: sales ledger debit/credit balances, purchases ledger debit/credit balances — 5

- identify discrepancies between the sales and purchases ledger control accounts and the individual ledgers — 5

- identify reasons for discrepancies between the sales and purchases ledger control accounts and the individual ledgers. — 5

4 Use the journal

4.1 Produced journal entries to record accounting transactions

Students need to be able to:

- record opening entries for a new business — 4

- identify and record entries to write off irrecoverable debts: record VAT — 4

- identify and record entries for payroll transactions: wages control account, gross pay, income tax, employer's and employees' national insurance contributions (NIC), employer's and employees' pension and voluntary deductions. — 6

4.2 Produce journal entries to correct errors not disclosed by the trial balance

Students need to be able to:

- correct errors using the journal: errors of commission, errors of omission, errors of original entry, errors of principle, reversal of entries, compensating errors.

4

4.3 Produce journal entries to correct errors disclosed by the trial balance

Students need to be able to:

- open a suspense account

- correct errors and clear the suspense account using the journal.

4

4.4 Use journal entries to make adjustments in the ledger accounts

Students need to be able to:

- post journal entries to the general ledger accounts

3

- total and balance the general ledger accounts: balance carried down, balance brought down.

3

4.5 Redraft the trial balance following adjustments

Students need to be able to:

- recalculate the balance of a general ledger account following journal entries

3

- complete a trial balance from adjusted and unadjusted balances

3

- balance the adjusted trial balance: total debit and credit columns.

3

5 Reconcile a bank statement with the cash book

5.1 Locate differences between items on the bank statement and entries in the cash book

Students need to be able to:

- recognise items on the bank statement but not in the cash book and recognise items in the cash book but not on the bank statement: opening balance differences, bank interest paid/received, bank charges, automated payments/receipts, unpresented cheques and outstanding lodgements.   7

5.2 Use the bank statement to update the cash book

Students need to be able to:

- make appropriate entries from the bank statement into the cash book: bank interest paid/received, bank charges and automated payments/receipts   7

- total and balance the cash book: credit/debit balance carried down, credit/debit balance brought down.   7

5.3 Produce a bank reconciliation statement

Students need to be able to:

- use appropriate items to complete a bank reconciliation statement: closing bank statement credit balance, unpresented cheques, outstanding lodgements   7

- check a bank statement has been correctly reconciled with a (debit) closing cash book balance.   7

KAPLAN PUBLISHING

Delivering this unit

Unit name	Content links	Suggested order of delivery
Bookkeeping Transactions	This unit builds on the knowledge and skills acquired from studying Bookkeeping Transactions, in particular double-entry bookkeeping techniques and reconciliation processes.	It is recommended that Bookkeeping Controls is delivered either after, or at the same time as Bookkeeping Transactions.
Using Accounting Software	Prior completion of both Level 2 manual bookkeeping units will benefit students studying Using Accounting Software. The skills and knowledge gained will enable students to understand the business environment and facilitate their comprehension of a computerised accounting system.	It is recommended that Bookkeeping Controls is delivered either before, or at the same time as Using Accounting Software.

THE ASSESSMENT

Test specification for this unit assessment

Assessment type	Marking type	Duration of exam
Computer based unit assessment	Computer marked	2 hours

The assessment for this unit consists of 10 compulsory, independent, tasks.

The competency level for AAT assessment is 70%.

Learning outcomes		Weighting
1	Understand payment methods	5%
2	Understand controls in a bookkeeping system	5%
3	Use control accounts	20%
4	Use the journal	50%
5	Reconcile bank statement with the cash book	20%
Total		100%

KAPLAN PUBLISHING

UNIT LINK TO SYNOPTIC ASSESSMENT

AAT AQ16 introduced a Synoptic Assessment, which students must complete if they are to achieve the appropriate qualification upon completion of a qualification. In the case of the Foundation Diploma in Accounting, students must pass all of the mandatory assessments and the Synoptic Assessment to achieve the qualification.

As a Synoptic Assessment is attempted following completion of individual units, it draws upon knowledge and understanding from those units. It may be appropriate for students to retain their study materials for individual units until they have successfully completed the Synoptic Assessment for that qualification.

With specific reference to this unit, the following learning objectives are also relevant to the Foundation Diploma in Accounting Synoptic Assessment

LO3 Use control accounts

LO4 Use the journal

LO5 Reconcile a bank statement with the cash book

Terminology

Students should be familiar with IFRS terminology. Other terms are used in this document to match titles provided by the QCF.

Also note, under payroll the terms 'PAYE' and 'National Insurance Contributions (NIC)' may also be known as 'Income Tax' and 'Social Security' respectively.

STUDY SKILLS

Preparing to study

Devise a study plan

Determine which times of the week you will study.

Split these times into sessions of at least one hour for study of new material. Any shorter periods could be used for revision or practice.

Put the times you plan to study onto a study plan for the weeks from now until the assessment and set yourself targets for each period of study – in your sessions make sure you cover the whole course, activities and the associated questions in the study text at the back of the manual.

If you are studying more than one unit at a time, try to vary your subjects as this can help to keep you interested and see subjects as part of wider knowledge.

When working through your course, compare your progress with your plan and, if necessary, re-think your work (perhaps including extra sessions) or, if you are ahead, do some extra revision / practice questions.

Effective studying

Active reading

You are not expected to learn the text by rote, rather, you must understand what you are reading and be able to use it to pass the assessment and develop good practice.

A good technique is to use SQ3Rs – Survey, Question, Read, Recall, Review:

1   **Survey the chapter**

    Look at the headings and read the introduction, knowledge, skills and content, so as to get an overview of what the chapter deals with.

2   **Question**

    Whilst undertaking the survey ask yourself the questions you hope the chapter will answer for you.

KAPLAN PUBLISHING

3   Read

Read through the chapter thoroughly working through the activities.

4   Recall

At the end of each section and at the end of the chapter, try to recall the main ideas of the section/chapter without referring to the text. This is best done after short break of a couple of minutes after the reading stage.

5   Review

Check that your recall notes are correct.

You may also find it helpful to re-read the chapter to try and see the topic(s) it deals with as a whole.

Note taking

Taking notes is a useful way of learning, but do not simply copy out the text.

The notes must:

- be in your own words

- be concise

- cover the key points

- be well organised

- be modified as you study further chapters in this text or in related ones.

Trying to summarise a chapter without referring to the text can be a useful way of determining which areas you know and which you don't.

Three ways of taking notes

1   Summarise the key points of a chapter

2   Make linear notes

A list of headings, subdivided with sub-headings listing the key points.

If you use linear notes, you can use different colours to highlight key points and keep topic areas together.

Use plenty of space to make your notes easy to use.

3 **Try a diagrammatic form**

The most common of which is a mind map.

To make a mind map, put the main heading in the centre of the paper and put a circle around it.

Draw lines radiating from this to the main sub-headings which again have circles around them.

Continue the process from the sub-headings to sub-sub-headings.

Annotating the text

You may find it useful to underline or highlight key points in your study text – but do be selective.

You may also wish to make notes in the margins.

Revision phase

Kaplan has produced material specifically designed for your final assessment preparation for this unit.

These include pocket revision notes and a bank of revision questions specifically in the style of the new syllabus.

Further guidance on how to approach the final stage of your studies is given in these materials.

Further reading

In addition to this text, you should also read the 'Accounting Technician' magazine every month to keep abreast of any guidance from the examiners.

Re-cap: Accounting for sales

1

Introduction

You previously studied the double entry bookkeeping for sales and receipts in detail within Bookkeeping Transactions. It is essential that you have completed your Bookkeeping Transactions studies commencing your studies for Bookkeeping Controls.

When studying Bookkeeping Transactions you concentrated on the basic accounting entries so that the double entry would be clear. It is now time to build on these basic entries and study these transactions again using more realistic material.

ASSESSMENT CRITERIA
• N/A – Underpinning knowledge from Bookkeeping Transactions

CONTENTS

1 The sales day book
2 The analysed sales day book
3 The sales returns day book
4 Posting to the sales ledger
5 The analysed cash book
6 The two column cash book
7 Discounts

1   The sales day book

1.1   Introduction

The sales day book is a book of prime entry where credit sales are recorded. Rather than produce a double entry every time a sale is made, these are instead recorded into a sales day book.

From invoices, items will be split into the gross, net and VAT amounts. This is because the three items are treated differently.

- The full total of the invoice is taken to the 'Total' column.

- The VAT amount is taken to the 'VAT' column (Remember that VAT is calculated net of all discounts).

- The net amount is taken to the 'Net' column.

The total at the end of the period is then posted into the accounts as follows:

Dr   Sales ledger control account (SLCA)   X

      Cr   Sales revenue   X

      Cr   VAT   X

The full (gross) amount is taken to the SLCA, as the customer owes the full amount. The net amount (the amount before VAT is added) is taken to sales revenue, as this is the amount the company can keep. The VAT amount is held as a liability, as this amount is due to be paid over to HMRC.

While Bookkeeping Controls does not require the posting of individual sales or purchase invoices into day books, the knowledge of the double entry is key. The assessment will assume this knowledge, and it will become very important in later chapters when errors and journals are considered.

KAPLAN PUBLISHING

The following example provides us with a recap of the material from our Bookkeeping Transactions studies.

 Example 1

Given below are three invoices that have been sent out by your organisation today. You are required to record them in the sales day book

INVOICE

Invoice to:
T J Builder
142/148 Broadway
Oldham
OD7 6LZ

Deliver to:
As above

A.J. Broom & Company Limited

59 Parkway
Manchester
M2 6EG
Tel: 0161 560 3392
Fax: 0161 560 5322

Invoice no:	69489
Tax point:	23 August 20X3
VAT reg no:	625 9911 58
Delivery note no:	68612
Account no:	SL21

Code	Description	Quantity	VAT rate	Unit price	Amount excl of VAT
			%	£	£
874 KL7	Brown Brick Roof Tiles	40	20	41.75	1,670.00
					1,670.00
VAT					334.00
Total amount payable					2,004.00

INVOICE

Invoice to:
McCarthy & Sons
Shepherds Moat
Manchester M6 9LF

Deliver to:
As above

A.J. Broom & Company Limited

59 Parkway
Manchester
M2 6EG
Tel: 0161 560 3392
Fax: 0161 560 5322

Invoice no:	69490
Tax point:	28 August 20X3
VAT reg no:	625 9911 58
Delivery note no:	68610
Account no:	SL08

Code	Description	Quantity	VAT rate	Unit price	Amount excl of VAT
			%	£	£
617 BB8	Red Wall Bricks	400	20	2.00	800.00
294 KT6	Insulation Brick	3	20	146.04	438.12
					1,238.12
VAT					247.62
Total amount payable					1,485.74

INVOICE

A.J. Broom & Company Limited

Invoice to:
Trevor Partner
Anderson House
Bank Street
Manchester M1 9FP

59 Parkway
Manchester
M2 6EG
Tel: 0161 560 3392
Fax: 0161 560 5322

Deliver to:
As above

Invoice no:	69491
Tax point:	28 August 20X3
VAT reg no:	625 9911 58
Delivery note no:	68613
Account no:	SL10

Code	Description	Quantity	VAT rate	Unit price	Amount excl of VAT
			%	£	£
611 TB4	Bathroom Tiles	160	20	5.54	886.40
					886.40
VAT					177.28
Total amount payable					1063.68

Solution

SALES DAY BOOK						
Date	Invoice No	Customer name	Code	Total £	VAT £	Net £
28/08/X3	69489	T J Builder	SL21	2,004.00	334.00	1,670.00
28/08/X3	69490	McCarthy & Sons	SL08	1,485.74	247.62	1,238.12
28/08/X3	69491	Trevor Partner	SL10	1,063.68	177.28	886.40

2 The analysed sales day book

2.1 Introduction

Many organisations analyse their sales into different groups. This may be analysis by different products or by the geographical area in which the sale is made. If the sales are eventually to be analysed in this manner in the accounting records then they must be analysed in the original book of prime entry, the sales day book.

Again, in Bookkeeping Controls you will not be required to produce an analysed day book. However, it is possible that you will be given an analysed day book as part of the information for you to use, so it is important that you are familiar with how it looks.

 Example 2

You work for an organisation that makes sales to five different geographical regions. You are in charge of writing up the sales day book and you have listed out the details of the invoices sent out yesterday, 15 August 20X1. They are given below and must be entered into the sales day book and the totals of each column calculated. The VAT rate in use is 20%.

The invoice details are as follows:

	£
Invoice number 167 – Scotland	
Worldwide News – (Code W5)	
Net total	2,500.00
VAT	500.00
Gross	3,000.00
Invoice number 168 – North	
Local News – (Code L1)	
Net total	200.00
VAT	40.00
Gross	240.00

Invoice number 169 – South	
The Press Today – (Code P2)	
Net total	300.00
VAT	60.00
	———
Gross	360.00
	———
Invoice number 170 – North	
Home Call – (Code H1)	
Net total	200.00
VAT	40.00
	———
Gross	240.00
	———
Invoice number 171 – Scotland	
Tomorrow – (Code T1)	
Net total	100.00
VAT	20.00
	———
Gross	120.00
	———
Invoice number 172 – East	
Worldwide News – (Code W5)	
Net total	3,000.00
VAT	600.00
	———
Gross	3,600.00
	———

Solution

SALES DAY BOOK										
Date	Invoice no	Customer name	Code	Total	VAT	East	West	North	South	Scotland
				£	£	£	£	£	£	£
15/08/X1	167	Worldwide	W5	3,000.00	500.00					2,500.00
	168	Local News	L1	240.00	40.00			200.00		
	169	The Press Today	P2	360.00	60.00				300.00	
	170	Home Call	H1	240.00	40.00			200.00		
	171	Tomorrow	T1	120.00	20.00					100.00
	172	Worldwide News	W5	3,600.00	600.00	3,000.00				
				7,560.00	1,260.00	3,000.00	–	400.00	300.00	2,600.00

When you have totalled the columns you can check your additions by 'cross-casting'. If you add together the totals of all of the analysis columns and the VAT column, they should total the figure in the 'Total' column.

 Test your understanding 1

Sweepings Ltd is a wall covering manufacturer. It produces four qualities of wallpaper:

01 – Anaglypta

02 – Supaglypta

03 – Lincrusta

04 – Blown Vinyl

Francis is a sales ledger clerk and he is required to write up the sales day book each week from the batch of sales invoices he receives from the sales department.

He has just received this batch of sales invoices which show the following details. All sales are standard-rated for VAT.

Invoice no	Date	Customer	Description	Amount (incl VAT) £
1700	06.09.X1	Gates Stores	Anaglypta, 188 rolls	480.00
1701	06.09.X1	Texas	Blown Vinyl, 235 rolls	1,800.00
1702	07.09.X1	Dickens	Blown Vinyl, 188 rolls	1,440.00
1703	07.09.X1	Hintons DIY	Supaglypta, 470 rolls	1,920.00
1704	08.09.X1	Co-op Stores	Anaglypta, 94 rolls	240.00
1705	08.09.X1	B & Q Stores	Lincrusta, 125 rolls	1,200.00
1706	09.09.X1	Ferris Decor	Supaglypta, 235 rolls	960.00
1707	09.09.X1	Ferris Decor	Blown Vinyl, 94 rolls	720.00
1708	10.09.X1	Homestyle	Lincrusta, 25 rolls	240.00
1709	10.09.X1	Quick Style	Anaglypta, 47 rolls	120.00

Show how this information would appear in the sales day book given below, including the totals of the relevant columns.

SALES DAY BOOK									
Date	Invoice	Customer	Code	Total	VAT	Group 01	Group 02	Group 03	Group 04
				£	£	£	£	£	£

Test your understanding 2

Given below are the totals from the analysed sales day book for an organisation for a week.

Sales day book

	Gross	VAT	Sales – Type 1	Sales – Type 2
	£	£	£	£
Totals	8,652.00	1,442.00	4,320.00	2,890.00

You are required to post these totals to the general ledger accounts given below: SLCA account

SLCA account

	£		£

Sales – Type 1 account

	£		£

Sales – Type 2 account

	£		£

VAT account

	£		£

3 The sales returns day book

3.1 Introduction

When goods are returned by customers and credit notes sent out then these credit notes are also recorded in their own book of prime entry, the sales returns day book.

3.2 Sales returns day book

The sales returns day book is effectively the reverse of the sales day book but will have the same entries, the total of the credit note, including VAT, the VAT element and the net amount, excluding the VAT.

Example 3

Given below are the totals from three credit notes that your organisation has sent out this week, the week ending 21 January 20X4. They are to be recorded in the sales returns day book.

Credit note no:	03556	To: J Slater & Co	Code: SL67
		£	
Goods total		126.45	
VAT		25.29	
Credit note total		151.74	

Credit note no:	03557	To: Paulsons	Code: SL14
		£	
Goods total		58.40	
VAT		11.68	
Credit note total		70.08	

Credit note no:	03558	To: Hudson & Co	Code: SL27
		£	
Goods total		104.57	
VAT		20.91	
Credit note total		125.48	

Solution

Sales returns day book

Date	Credit note no	Customer name	Code	Total £	VAT £	Net £
21/01/X4	03556	J Slater & Co	SL67	151.74	25.29	126.45
21/01/X4	03557	Paulsons	SL14	70.08	11.68	58.40
21/01/X4	03558	Hudson & Co	SL27	125.48	20.91	104.57

3.3 Analysed sales returns day book

If the business keeps an analysed sales day book then it will also analyse its sales returns day book in exactly the same manner.

Example 4

In an earlier example we considered the sales day book for an organisation that makes sales to five different geographical regions. The sales returns day book would also be analysed into these geographical regions. The details of two credit notes issued this week are given and are to be written up in the sales returns day book. Today's date is 21 October 20X6.

Credit note no: 0246 – West	To: Russell & Sons	Code: R03
	£	
Goods total	85.60	
VAT	17.12	
	102.72	

Credit note no: 0247 – South   To: Cleansafe   Code: C07

	£
Goods total	126.35
VAT	25.27
	151.62

Solution

Sales returns day book

Date	Credit	Customer	Code	Total	VAT	East	West	North	South	Scotland
21/10/X6	0246	Russell & Sons	R03	102.72	17.12		85.60			
21/10/X6	0247	Cleansafe	C07	151.62	25.27				126.35	

Test your understanding 3

A business analyses its sales into Product 1 sales and Product 2 sales. During the week ending 14 March 20X4 the following credit notes were sent out to customers.

CN3066	£120.00 plus VAT	–	Product 2, Customer K Lilt, Code L04
CN3067	£16.00 plus VAT	–	Product 1, Customer J Davis, Code D07
CN3068	£38.00 plus VAT	–	Product 1, Customer I Oliver, Code O11
CN3069	£80.00 plus VAT	–	Product 2, Customer D Sharp, Code S02

Enter the credit notes in the analysed sales returns day book given below and total the day book for the week.

Sales returns day book

Date	Credit note no	Customer name	Code	Total	VAT	Product 1	Product 2
				£	£	£	£

Test your understanding 4

Given below are the totals from the analysed sales returns day book for an organisation for a week:

Date	Customer name	Credit note no	Code	Total	VAT	Sales Type 1	Sales Type 2
				£	£	£	£
25/09/X2				601.80	100.30	327.00	174.50

Post these totals to the general ledger accounts.

Sales ledger control account

£	£

Sales returns – Type 1

£	£

Sales returns – Type 2

£	£

VAT account

£	£

4 Posting to the sales ledger

As well as posting the totals from the books of prime entry to the general ledger accounts each individual invoice and credit note must also be posted to the individual customer's account in the sales ledger. You must remember that the sales ledger is sometimes referred to as the subsidiary sales ledger.

Remember that the subsidiary ledgers are **NOT** part of the double entry system. They merely split up the balance in the SLCA between individual customers so that companies can keep track of the amounts owed to them by specific customers.

As well as having the subsidiary ledgers, it is important for the business to maintain an aged receivables ledger. This will ensure that the business is able to see which receivables are not paying on time. This will enable the business to contact the customer and request payment to prevent this becoming an irrecoverable debt, which is discussed further in chapter 4.

Example 5

Here is an account from the sales ledger of Frosty Limited, a glass manufacturer which specialises in glassware for the catering trade.

Account name:		Account code:	
	£		£

You have taken over writing up the sales ledger because the ledger clerk has been ill for several months.

You have gathered together the following information about sales. The customer is a new customer whose name is Arthur Pickering. The account code will be SP05.

Sales invoices

Date	Invoice number	Gross	VAT	Net
		£	£	£
02/05/X1	325	598.06	99.67	498.39
03/06/X1	468	243.98	40.66	203.32
15/06/X1	503	115.84	19.30	96.54
16/06/X1	510	49.74	8.29	41.45
24/06/X1	CN048	28.32	4.72	23.60
17/07/X1	604	450.51	75.08	375.43

Solution

Account name: Arthur Pickering   Account code: SP05

		£			£
02/05/X1	Inv 325	598.06	25/06/X1	CN048	28.32
03/06/X1	Inv 468	243.98			
15/06/X1	Inv 503	115.84			
16/06/X1	Inv 510	49.74			
17/07/X1	Inv 604	450.51			

Remember that sales invoices are always entered on the debit side of the customer's account and credit notes on the credit side of the account.

5 The analysed cash book

5.1 Introduction

In order to revise the layout of the cash receipts book consider the following example.

Cash receipts book for the week commencing 15 September 20X4

Date	Narrative	Total	VAT	SLCA	Cash/ cheque sales
		£	£	£	£
15 Sept	Paying-in slip 584	653.90		653.90	
16 Sept	Paying-in slip 585	864.60		864.60	
17 Sept	Paying-in slip 586	954.98	11.24	887.54	56.20
18 Sept	Paying-in slip 587	559.57		559.57	
19 Sept	Paying-in slip 588	238.18	31.69	48.00	158.49
		3,271.23	42.93	3,013.61	214.69

The bankings are a mixture of cash sales and cheques from receivables. The VAT is just the VAT on the cash/cheque sales.

Check that the three analysis column totals add back to the total column total.

Example 6

Returning to the cash receipts book, post the totals to the general ledger accounts.

Cash receipts book

Date	Narrative	Total	VAT	Receiv-ables	Cash/cheque sales
		£	£	£	£
15 Sept	Paying-in slip 584	653.90		653.90	
16 Sept	Paying-in slip 585	864.60		864.60	
17 Sept	Paying-in slip 586	954.98	11.24	887.54	56.20
18 Sept	Paying-in slip 587	559.57		559.57	
19 Sept	Paying-in slip 588	238.18	31.69	48.00	158.49
		3,271.23	42.93	3,013.61	214.69

Solution

The double entry for posting the cash receipts book totals is:

		£	£
Dr	Bank account	3,271.23	
Cr	VAT account		42.93
	Sales ledger control account		3,013.61
	Sales account		214.69

Bank account

	£		£
Cash receipts book (CRB)	3,271.23		

VAT account

	£		£
		CRB	42.93

Sales ledger control account

	£		£
		CRB	3,013.61

Sales

	£		£
		CRB	214.69

6 The two column cash book

6.1 Introduction

Within Bookkeeping Transactions, the analysed cash receipts book and cash payments book were looked at separately.

A 'two column' cash book is the terminology used when the cash book details cash and bank transactions.

Test your understanding 5

Cash book – Debit side

Date	Details	Bank £
30 Nov	Balance b/d	10,472
30 Nov	SMK Ltd	12,000

(a) What will be the ONE entry in the sales ledger?

Sales ledger

Account name	Amount £	Debit/Credit

(b) What will be the ONE entry in the general ledger?

General ledger

Account name	Amount £	Debit/Credit

7 Discounts

A discount is a reduction to the price of the sales of goods or services. There are different types of discounts that may be offered for different reasons.

 Definition – Trade discount

A trade discount is a definite amount that is deducted from the list price of the goods for the supplies to some customers, with the intention of encouraging and rewarding customer loyalty.

 Definition – Bulk discount

A bulk discount is similar to a trade discount in that it is deducted from the list price of the goods and disclosed on the invoice. However, a bulk discount is given by a supplier for sales orders above a certain quantity.

 Definition – Prompt payment discount

Prompt payment discounts (also known as settlement or cash discounts) are offered to customers in order to encourage early payment of invoices.

A trade discount or a bulk discount is a definite reduction in price from the list price whereas a prompt payment discount is only a reduction in price if the organisation decides to take advantage of it by making early payment.

VAT calculations and discounts

VAT is calculated after trade and bulk discounts have been deducted from the original list price.

Prompt payment discounts are only offered on an invoice so it does not impact the VAT calculation at the point of the invoice preparation.

If the customer goes on to take advantage of a prompt payment discount offered, the VAT amount is adjusted.

Example 7

L sells £1,000 of goods net of VAT (at 20%) to M on credit. There is an agreed 10% trade discount with M. Enter these transactions in the accounts.

Solution

Step 1   Calculate the VAT on the sale.

	£
Original list price of goods	1,000.00
Less: 10% trade discount	(100.00)
Net invoice value	900.00
VAT (20% × £900)	180.00
Total (gross) invoice value	1,080.00

Step 2   Enter the invoice in the accounts.

Receivables

	£		£
Sales and VAT	1,080.00		

Sales

	£		£
		Receivables	900.00

VAT

	£		£
		Receivables	180.00

Prompt payment discounts

Prompt payment VAT legislation was amended (Revenue and Customs Brief 49 (2014)) and the changes took effect from 1 April 2015. The AAT have made these changes examinable for Bookkeeping Controls from September 2016.

Although a customer may be offered a prompt payment discount no reflection of this discount is shown within the accounting records until the customer does take advantage of this, if they choose to do so. When initially raising an invoice, VAT should be charged on the full price of the goods or services (although this would be after deducting trade or bulk discounts).

If the customer takes advantage of the prompt payment discount the VAT would be adjusted to reflect the discount taken. This adjustment could be by way of a credit note - the chosen method for the Bookkeeping Controls assessment criteria. The credit note to reflect this prompt payment discount is entered into the discounts allowed day book (DADB).

 Example 8

Leo, a trader, sells goods for £500 (exclusive of VAT). He offers a 10% discount if payment is made within 7 days.

The amounts shown as due on the invoice will be:

Sales price	£500
VAT	£100
Amount due	£600

The invoice will state that a prompt payment discount of £60 can be deducted from the amount due if payment is made within 7 days. If the trader takes the discount the supplier must then issue a credit note for £60 i.e. £50 + VAT of £10. This credit note will be recorded in the discounts allowed day book.

To summarise, the accounting entries for a prompt payment discount are:

Debit	Discounts allowed account with the net amount
Debit	VAT account with the VAT amount
Credit	Receivable account with the gross amount

The gross amount is credited to the receivables account. This is recognising the reduction to the receivable of the discount and associated VAT charge.

The net amount is debited to the discounts allowed account. This is recognising an expense of allowing a discount. Note that this is for the VAT exclusive amount.

The VAT amount based on the discount allowed is debited to the VAT account in recognition that this amount is no longer owed to HMRC as there has been a reduction to the original price due to the customer taking advantage of a settlement discount.

Test your understanding 6

Given below are the details of paying-in slip 609 from Passiflora Products Ltd. You are required to enter the details in the sales ledger accounts given.

Paying-in slip 609

	Amount	Discount allowed
	£	£
Natural Beauty	11,797.05	176.95
Grapeseed	417.30	6.26
New Age Remedies	6,379.65	95.69
The Aromatherapy Shop	9,130.65	136.96

Natural Beauty

	£		£
Opening balance	17,335.24		

The Aromatherapy Shop

	£		£
Opening balance	12,663.42		

New Age Remedies

	£		£
Opening balance	6,475.34		

Grapeseed

	£		£
Opening balance	423.56		

8 Summary

In this chapter we have pulled together into one place all the main documents and double entry for the sales cycle. If you have had any trouble with any of these points, you should refer again to the relevant chapters of the textbook for Bookkeeping Transactions where the double entry is explained in basic terms. Bookkeeping Controls builds onto our knowledge from Bookkeeping Transactions.

Test your understanding answers

Test your understanding 1

SALES DAY BOOK

Date	Invoice	Customer	Code	Total	VAT	Group 01	Group 02	Group 03	Group 04
				£	£	£	£	£	£
06/09/X1	1700	Gates Stores		480.00	80.00	400.00			
06/09/X1	1701	Texas		1,800.00	300.00				1,500.00
07/09/X1	1702	Dickens		1,440.00	240.00				1,200.00
07/09/X1	1703	Hintons DIY		1,920.00	320.00		1,600.00		
08/09/X1	1704	Co-op Stores		240.00	40.00	200.00			
08/09/X1	1705	B & Q Stores		1,200.00	200.00			1,000.00	
09/09/X1	1706	Ferris Decor		960.00	160.00		800.00		
09/09/X1	1707	Ferris Decor		720.00	120.00				600.00
10/09/X1	1708	Homestyle		240.00	40.00			200.00	
10/09/X1	1709	Quick Style		120.00	20.00	100.00			
				9,120.00	1,520.00	700.00	2,400.00	1,200.00	3,300.00

Test your understanding 2

SLCA

	£		£
SDB	8,652.00		

Sales – Type 1 account

	£		£
		SDB	4,320.00

Sales – Type 2 account

	£		£
		SDB	2,890.00

VAT account

	£		£
		SDB	1,442.00

Test your understanding 3

SALES RETURNS DAY BOOK

Date	Credit note	Customer name	Code	Total £	VAT £	Product 1 £	Product 2 £
14/3/X4	3066	K Lilt	L04	144.00	24.00		120.00
14/3/X4	3067	J Davis	D07	19.20	3.20	16.00	
14/3/X4	3068	I Oliver	O11	45.60	7.60	38.00	
14/3/X4	3069	D Sharp	S02	96.00	16.00		80.00
				304.80	50.80	54.00	200.00

Test your understanding 4

Sales ledger control account

	£		£
		SRDB	601.80

Sales returns – Type 1

	£		£
SRDB	327.00		

Sales returns – Type 2

	£		£
SRDB	174.50		

VAT account

	£		£
SRDB	100.30		

Test your understanding 5

Sales ledger

Account name	Amount £	Debit/Credit
SMK Ltd	12,000	Credit

General ledger

Account name	Amount £	Debit/Credit
SLCA	12,000	Credit

Test your understanding 6

Natural Beauty

	£		£
Opening balance	17,335.24	CRB	11,797.05
		DADB – discount	176.95

The Aromatherapy Shop

	£		£
Opening balance	12,663.42	CRB	9,130.65
		DADB – discount	136.96

New Age Remedies

	£		£
Opening balance	6,475.34	CRB	6,379.65
		DADB – discount	95.69

Grapeseed

	£		£
Opening balance	423.56	CRB	417.30
		DADB – discount	6.26

Re-cap: Accounting for purchases

2

Introduction

As well as recapping accounting for sales as seen in chapter 1, we also need to re-cap on the techniques learned in Bookkeeping Transactions for purchases.

ASSESSMENT CRITERIA
• N/A – Underpinning knowledge from Bookkeeping Transactions

CONTENTS

1 The purchases day book
2 Returns of goods
3 Accounting entries in the general ledger
4 Accounting entries in the purchases ledger
5 The impact of VAT
6 Discounts
7 The two column cashbook

1 The purchases day book

1.1 Introduction

The purchases day book works the same way as the sales day book. All credit purchases for the period are listed, and then the totals for that period are recorded into the ledgers.

The total (gross) amount goes to the purchase ledger control account (PLCA), as the supplier is owed the full amount.

The net amount (before VAT) is recorded in purchases, as this is what the goods will ultimately cost the company, as the VAT element can be reclaimed.

The VAT amount is recorded as an asset, as the VAT on purchases of goods can be reclaimed from HMRC (assuming the company is registered for VAT).

The double entry is therefore:

Dr	Purchases	X (Net amount)
Dr	VAT	X (VAT amount)
	Cr Purchase ledger control account	X (Full amount)

1.2 Authorisation stamp

To ensure that only valid purchases are made by the business, and to ensure only real invoices are accepted, senior staff members should authorise the invoices as they arrive.

This is often done by stamping an authorisation stamp or grid stamp onto the invoice once it has been thoroughly checked and the relevant details entered onto the authorisation stamp. A typical example of an authorisation stamp is shown below:

Purchase order no	04618
Invoice no	04821
Cheque no	
Account code	PL06
Checked	L Finn
Date	23/02/X2
GL account	07

KAPLAN PUBLISHING

1.3 Entries on the authorisation stamp

The purchase order number is entered onto the authorisation stamp.

The purchase invoice will then be allocated an internal invoice number which will be sequential and therefore the next number after the last invoice entered into the purchases day book.

The purchase invoice details, such as trade and settlement discounts should have been checked to the supplier's file to ensure that the correct percentages have been used and at this point the supplier's purchases ledger code can be entered onto the authorisation stamp.

The person checking the invoice should then sign and date the authorisation stamp to show that all details have been checked.

Finally, the general ledger account code should be entered. We have seen that in some businesses a simple three column purchases day book will be used with a total, VAT and net column. In such cases all of the invoices will be classified as 'purchases' and will have the general ledger code for the purchases account.

However, if an analysed purchases day book is used then each analysis column will be for a different type of expense and will have a different general ledger code.

If your organisation does have an authorisation stamp procedure then it is extremely important that the authorisation is correctly filled out when the invoice has been checked. Not only is this evidence that the invoice is correct and is for goods or services that have been received, it also provides vital information for the accurate accounting for this invoice.

Example 1

Given below are three purchase invoices received and the authorisation stamp for each one. They are to be entered into the purchases day book. Today's date is 25 April 20X1.

INVOICE

Invoice to:
Keller Bros
Field House
Winstead
M16 4PT

Anderson Wholesale
Westlife Park
Gripton
M7 1ZK
Tel: 0161 439 2020
Fax: 0161 439 2121

Deliver to:
Above address

Invoice no:	06447
Tax point:	20 April 20X1
VAT reg no:	432 1679 28
Account no:	SL14

Code	Description	Quantity	VAT rate	Unit price	Amount excl VAT
			%	£	£
PT417	Grade A Compost	7 tonnes	20	15.01	105.07
					105.07
VAT					21.01
Total amount payable					126.08

Purchase order no	34611
Invoice no	37240 (internal)
Cheque no	
Account code	PL14
Checked	C Long
Date	25/04/X1
GL account	020

INVOICE

Invoice to:
Keller Bros
Field House
Winstead
M16 4PT

Deliver to:
Above address

Better Gardens Ltd
Broom Nursery
West Lane
Farforth M23 4LL
Tel: 0161 380 4444
Fax: 0161 380 6128

Invoice no:	46114
Tax point:	21 April 20X1
VAT reg no:	611 4947 26
Account no:	K03

Code	Description	Quantity	VAT rate	Unit price	Amount excl VAT
			%	£	£
B4188	Tulip bulbs	28 dozen	20	1.34	37.52
B3682	Daffodil bulbs	50 dozen	20	1.22	61.00
					98.52
VAT					19.70
Total amount payable					118.22

Purchase order no	34608
Invoice no	37241 (internal)
Cheque no	
Account code	PL06
Checked	C Long
Date	25/04/X1
GL account	020

INVOICE

Invoice to:
Keller Bros
Field House
Winstead
M16 4PT

Winterton Partners
28/32 Coleman Road
Forest Dene
M17 3AT
Tel: 0161 224 6760
Fax: 0161 224 6761

Deliver to:
Above address

Invoice no:	121167
Tax point:	22 April 20X1
VAT reg no:	980 3012 74
Account no:	SL44

Code	Description	Quantity	Sales tax rate	Unit price	Amount excl VAT
			%	£	£
A47BT	Seedlings	120	20	0.69	82.80
VAT					16.56
Total amount payable					99.36

Purchase order no	34615
Invoice no	37242 (internal)
Cheque no	
Account code	PL23
Checked	C Long
Date	25/04/X1
GL account	020

Solution

Purchases day book						
Date	Invoice no	Code	Supplier	Total	VAT	Net
				£	£	£
25/04/X1	37240	PL14	Anderson Wholesale	126.08	21.01	105.07
25/04/X1	37241	PL06	Better Gardens Ltd	118.22	19.70	98.52
25/04/X1	37242	PL23	Winterton Partners	99.36	16.56	82.80

2 Returns of goods

2.1 Introduction

Returns may be made for various reasons, e.g.

- faulty goods
- excess goods delivered by supplier
- unauthorised goods delivered.

All returned goods must be recorded on a returns outwards note.

2.2 Credit notes

The return should not be recorded until the business receives a credit note from the supplier. This confirms that there is no longer a liability for these goods.

The credit note should be checked for accuracy against the returns outwards note. The calculations on the credit note should also be checked in just the same way as with an invoice.

2.3 Purchases returns day book

When credit notes are received from suppliers they are normally recorded in their own primary record, the purchases returns day book. This has a similar layout to a purchases day book. If the purchases day book is analysed into the different types of purchase that the organisation makes then the purchases returns day book will also be analysed in the same manner.

Example 2

Today, 5 February 20X5, three credit notes have been passed as being checked. The details of each credit note and the authorisation stamp are given below. The credit note details are to be entered into the purchases returns day book.

From Calderwood & Co	£
Goods total	16.80
VAT	3.36
Credit note total	20.16

Purchase order no	41120
Credit note	C461
Cheque no	–
Account code	053
Checked	J Garry
Date	05/02/X5
GL account	02

From Mellor & Cross	£
Goods total	94.05
VAT	18.81
Credit note total	112.86

Purchase order no	41096
Credit note	C462
Cheque no	–
Account code	259
Checked	J Garry
Date	05/02/X5
GL account	02

From Thompson Bros Ltd	**£**
Goods total	35.72
VAT	7.14
Credit note total	42.86

Purchase order no	41103
Credit note	C463
Cheque no	–
Account code	360
Checked	J Garry
Date	05/02/X5
GL account	01

Solution

Purchases returns day book

Date	Credit note no	Code	Supplier	Total £	VAT £	01 £	02 £	03 £	04 £
05/02/X5	C461	053	Calderwood & Co	20.16	3.36		16.80		
05/02/X5	C462	259	Mellor & Cross	112.86	18.81		94.05		
05/02/X5	C463	360	Thompson Bros Ltd	42.86	7.14	35.72			

Test your understanding 1

Write the invoices up in the purchases day book for a local newsagent. The last internal invoice number to be allocated to purchase invoices was 114.

1.1.X1	Northern Electric – invoice	£120 including VAT
	Northern Gas – invoice	£230 (no VAT)
2.1.X1	Post Office Ltd – invoice	£117.00 (no VAT)
	Northern Country – invoice	£48 including VAT
3.1.X1	South Gazette – invoice	£360 including VAT

The supplier codes are as follows:

Northern Country (a newspaper)	N1
Northern Electric	N2
Northern Gas	N3
Post Office Ltd	P1
South Gazette (a newspaper)	S1

Purchases day book

Date	Invoice no	Code	Supplier	Total	VAT	Goods for resale	Heat and light	Postage and stationery
				£	£	£	£	£

3 Accounting entries in the general ledger

3.1 Introduction

The accounting entries that are to be made in the general ledger are the same as those considered in Bookkeeping Transactions and are made from the totals of the columns in the purchases day book and purchases returns day book. These are outlined at the start of this chapter, and are crucial assumed knowledge for the Bookkeeping Controls assessment.

3.2 Analysed purchases day book

If an analysed purchases day book is being used then there will be a debit entry in an individual purchases or expense account for each of the analysis column totals.

Remember that these totals are the net of VAT purchases/expenses totals.

💡 Example 3

Reproduced below is a purchases day book for the first week of February 20X5. Each column has been totalled and it must be checked that the totals of the analysis columns agree to the 'Total' column. Therefore you should check the following sum:

	£
01	744.37
02	661.23
03	250.45
04	153.72
VAT	338.43
	2,148.20

Purchases day book

Date	Invoice no	Code	Supplier	Total £	VAT £	01 £	02 £	03 £	04 £
20X5									
1 Feb	3569	265	Norweb	151.44	25.24	126.20			
2 Feb	3570	053	Calderwood & Co	98.60			98.60		
3 Feb	3571	259	Mellor & Cross	675.15	112.52		562.63		
4 Feb	3572	360	Thompson Bros Ltd	265.71	44.28	221.43			
5 Feb	3573	023	Cooplin Associates	18.90				18.90	
	3574	056	Heywood Suppliers	277.86	46.31			231.55	
	3575	395	William Leggett	46.33	7.72				38.61
	3576	271	Melville Products	374.29	62.38	311.91			
	3577	301	Quick-Bake	101.79	16.96	84.83			
	3578	311	Roger & Roebuck	138.13	23.02				115.11
				2,148.20	338.43	744.37	661.23	250.45	153.72

The totals of the purchases day book will now be posted to the general ledger accounts.

Solution

Purchase ledger control account

	£			£
			PDB	2,148.20

VAT account

	£			£
PDB	338.43			

Purchases – 01 account

	£			£
PDB	744.37			

Purchases – 02 account

	£			£
PDB	661.23			

Purchases – 03 account

	£			£
PDB	250.45			

Purchases – 04 account

	£			£
PDB	153.72			

3.3 Purchases returns day book

The purchases returns day book is kept in order to record credit notes received by the business. The totals of this must also be posted to the general ledger.

 Example 4

Given below is a purchases returns day book for the week. The totals are to be posted to the general ledger accounts. VAT is at 20%.

Purchases day book									
Date	Credit note no	Code	Supplier	Total	VAT	01	02	03	04
				£	£	£	£	£	£
20X3									
4 May	CN 152	PL21	Julian R Partners	132.00	22.00		110.00		
6 May	CN 153	PL07	S T Trader	81.60	13.60			68.00	
8 May	CN 154	PL10	Ed Associates	70.32	11.72		58.60		
8 May	CN 155	PL03	Warren & Co	107.52	17.92	89.60			
				391.44	65.24	89.60	168.60	68.00	–

Solution

First, check that each of the column totals add back to the total column total:

	£
VAT	65.24
01	89.60
02	168.60
03	68.00
04	–
	391.44

Then post the totals to the general ledger accounts:

Purchases ledger control account

	£		£
Purchases return day book (PRDB)	391.44		

VAT account

	£		£
		PRDB	65.24

Purchases returns – 01

	£		£
		PRDB	89.60

Purchases returns – 02

	£		£
		PRDB	168.60

Purchases returns – 03

	£		£
		PRDB	68.00

If the purchases returns day book is analysed then there will be an account in the general ledger for each different category of purchases returns.

🖊 Test your understanding 2

Given below is the purchases day book. You are required to check the total of each analysis column and that the total of each analysis column agrees to the total column, and then to enter the totals in the correct general ledger accounts.

Purchases day book

Date	Invoice no	Code	Supplier	Total	VAT	Goods for sale	Heat and light	Postage and stationery
				£	£	£	£	£
01.01.X1	115	N2	Northern Electric	120.00	20.00		100.00	
	116	N3	Northern Gas	230.00			230.00	
02.01.X1	117	P1	Post Office	117.00				117.00
	118	N1	Northern Country	48.00	8.00	40.00		
03.01.X1	119	S1	South Gazette	360.00	60.00	300.00		
				875.00	88.00	340.00	330.00	117.00

4 Accounting entries in the purchases ledger

4.1 Purchases ledger

As well as posting the totals from the books of prime entry to the general ledger accounts, each individual invoice and credit note must also be posted to the individual supplier's account in the purchases ledger (also referred to as the subsidiary purchases ledger.

Remember that the subsidiary ledgers are **NOT** part of the double entry system. They merely split up the balance in the PLCA between individual suppliers so that companies can keep track of the amounts owed to specific suppliers.

Example 5

Here is an account from the purchases ledger of Frosty Limited.

Account name:			Code:		
Date	Transaction	£	Date	Transaction	£

We will write up the account for Jones Brothers, account number PJ06. This is a new supplier.

Frosty Limited has only been trading for a short time and is not yet registered for VAT.

Purchase invoices and credit notes

02.5.X1	9268	£638.26
06.6.X1	9369	£594.27
15.6.X1	9402	£368.24
17.6.X1	C Note 413	£58.62
19.6.X1	9568	£268.54

Solution

Account name: Jones Brothers   **Account number:** PJ06

Date	Transaction	£	Date	Transaction	£
17.6.X1	Credit note 413	58.62	02.5.X1	Invoice 9268	638.26
			06.6.X1	Invoice 9369	594.27
			15.6.X1	Invoice 9402	368.24
			19.6.X1	Invoice 9568	268.54

Each purchase invoice from the Purchases Day Book must be entered on the credit side of that individual suppliers account in the purchases ledger. Any credit notes recorded in the Purchases Returns Day Book must be recorded on the debit side of the supplier's account. Where there is VAT involved the amount to be recorded for an invoice or credit note is the gross amount or VAT inclusive amount.

5 The impact of VAT

5.1 Introduction

Having looked at the accounting for purchase invoices and credit notes, we will now move on to consider the accounting for payments to suppliers. First we will consider the impact of VAT in this area.

When writing up the payments side of the cash book VAT must be considered.

Any payments to suppliers or payables included in the Purchases ledger column need have no analysis for VAT as the VAT on the purchase was recorded in the purchases day book when the invoice was initially received.

However any other payments on which there is VAT must show the gross amount in the Total column, the VAT in the VAT column and the net amount in the relevant expense column.

Example 6

Peter Craddock is the cashier for a business which manufactures paper from recycled paper. The payments that were made for one week in September are as follows:

15 September	Cheque no 1151 to K Humphrey (credit supplier)	£1,034.67
	Cheque no 1152 to Y Ellis (credit supplier)	£736.45
	Cheque no 1153 to R Phipps (credit supplier)	£354.45
	Standing order for rent	£168.15
	Direct debit to the electricity company	£130.98
	(including VAT of £22.92)	
16 September	Cheque no 1154 to L Silton (credit supplier)	£1,092.75
	Cheque no 1155 to the insurance company	£103.18
17 September	Cheque no 1156 to F Grange (credit supplier)	£742.60
	Cheque no 1157 to Hettler Ltd for cash purchases	£420.00
	plus VAT	
18 September	Cheque no 1158 to J Kettle (credit supplier)	£131.89
19 September	BACS payment of wages	£4,150.09
	Cheque no 1159 to Krane Associates for cash purchases	£186.00
	plus VAT	

Enter these transactions into the cash payments book, total the columns and post the totals to the general ledger.

Solution

Date	Details	Cheque no	Total £	VAT £	PLCA £	Cash purchases £	Rent £	Electricity £	Wages £	Insurance £
15/9	K Humphrey	1151	1,034.67		1,034.67					
	Y Ellis	1152	736.45		736.45					
	R Phipps	1153	354.45		354.45					
	Rent	SO	168.15				168.15			
	Electricity	DD	130.98	22.92				108.06		
16/9	L Silton	1154	1,092.75		1,092.75					
	Insurance	1155	103.18							103.18
17/9	F Grange	1156	742.60		742.60					
	Hettler Ltd	1157	504.00	84.00		420.00				
18/9	J Kettle	1158	131.89		131.89					
	Wages	BACS	4,150.09						4,150.09	
19/9	Krane Ass	1159	223.20	37.20		186.00				
			9,372.41	144.12	4,092.81	606.00	168.15	108.06	4,150.09	103.18

The analysis column totals should add back to the Total column – this must always be done to check the accuracy of your totalling.

	£
VAT	144.12
Purchases ledger	4,092.81
Cash purchases	606.00
Rent	168.15
Electricity	108.06
Wages	4,150.09
Insurance	103.18
	9,372.41

Purchases ledger control account

		£			£
19/9	CPB	4,092.81			

VAT account

		£			£
19/9	CPB	144.12			

Purchases account

		£			£
19/9	CPB	606.00			

Electricity account

		£		£
19/9	CPB	108.06		

Wages account

		£		£
19/9	CPB	4,150.09		

Rent account

		£		£
19/9	CPB	168.15		

Insurance account

		£		£
19/9	CPB	103.18		

All of the entries in the general ledger accounts are debit entries. The credit entry is the total column of the cash payments book and these individual debit entries form the double entry.

6 Discounts

6.1 Introduction

VAT is calculated after trade and bulk discounts have been deducted from the original list price.

Prompt payment discounts are only offered on an invoice so it does not impact the VAT calculation at the point of the invoice preparation.

If the customer goes on to take advantage of a prompt payment discount offered, the VAT amount is adjusted. This adjustment could be by way of a credit note - the chosen method for the Bookkeeping Controls assessment criteria. The credit note to reflect this prompt payment discount is entered into the discounts received day book (DRDB).

The accounting entries for a prompt payment discount are:

Debit	Payables with the gross amount
Credit	VAT account with the VAT amount
Credit	Discounts received account with the net amount

Test your understanding 3

Given below is a completed cash payments book. You are required to:

(a) Total each of the columns and check that the totals add across to the total column.

(b) Post the totals to the general ledger accounts given.

(c) Post the individual payable entries to the payables' accounts in the purchases ledger, also given.

Date	Details	Cheque no	Code	Total £	VAT £	PLCA £	Cash purchases £	Wages £
1/7	G Hobbs	34	PL14	325.46		325.46		
1/7	Purchases	35	ML03	68.40	11.40		57.00	
2/7	Purchases	36	ML03	50.59	8.43		42.16	
3/7	P Taylor	37	PL21	157.83		157.83		
3/7	S Dent	38	PL06	163.58		163.58		
4/7	K Smith	39	ML07	24.56				24.56
				———	———	———	———	———
				———	———	———	———	———

(b) **General ledger accounts**

Purchases ledger control account

	£		£
CPB	646.87		

Cash purchases account

	£		£

Wages account

	£		£

VAT account

	£		£

(c)   **Purchases ledger**

G Hobbs			PL14
£			£

P Taylor			PL21
£			£

S Dent			PL06
£			£

7 The two column cashbook

7.1 Introduction

As we have revised receipts side the two column cashbook in the previous chapter, the following Test your understanding will revise this approach with the payments side.

Test your understanding 4

Cashbook – Credit side

Date	Details	VAT £	Bank £
30 Nov	Motor expenses	40	240
30 Nov	Wages		6,200
30 Nov	HMRC		4,750

What will be the FOUR entries in the general ledger?

General ledger

Account name	Amount £	Debit/Credit

8 Summary

In this chapter we have pulled together into one place all the main documents and double entry for the purchases cycle. If you have had any trouble with any of these points, you should refer again to the Bookkeeping Transactions Study Text where the double entry is explained.

Test your understanding answers

Test your understanding 1

Purchases day book

Date	Invoice no	Code	Supplier	Total	VAT	Goods for resale	Heat and light	Postage and stationery
				£	£	£	£	£
01.01.X1	115	N2	Northern Electric	120.00	20.00		100.00	
	116	N3	Northern Gas	230.00	–		230.00	
02/01.X1	117	P1	Post Office Ltd	117.00	–			117.00
	118	N1	Northern Country	48.00	8.00	40.00		
03/01/X1	119	S1	South Gazette	360.00	60.00	300.00		
				875.00	88.00	340.00	330.00	117.00

Test your understanding 2

	£
Goods for resale	340.00
Heat and light	330.00
Postage and stationery	117.00
VAT	88.00
Total	875.00

Purchases (goods for resale)

	£		£
PDB	340.00		

Heat and light

	£		£
PDB	330.00		

Postage and stationery

	£		£
PDB	117.00		

VAT

	£		£
PDB	88.00		

Purchases ledger control account

	£		£
		PDB	875.00

Test your understanding 3

(a)   Cash payments book

Date	Details	Cheque no	Code	Total	VAT	PLCA	Cash purchases	Wages
				£	£	£	£	£
1/7	G Hobbs	34	PL14	325.46		325.46		
1/7	Purchases	35	ML03	68.40	11.40		57.00	
2/7	Purchases	36	ML03	50.59	8.43		42.16	
3/7	P Taylor	37	PL21	157.83		157.83		
3/7	S Dent	38	PL06	163.58		163.58		
4/7	K Smith	39	ML07	24.56				24.56
				790.42	19.83	646.87	99.16	24.56

Check that totals add across:

	£
VAT	19.83
Purchases ledger	646.87
Cash purchases	99.16
Wages	24.56
	790.42

(b)   General ledger accounts

Purchases ledger control account

	£		£
CPB	646.87		

Cash purchases account

	£		£
CPB	99.16		

Wages account

	£		£
CPB	24.56		

VAT account

	£		£
CPB	19.83		

(c)   Purchases ledger

G Hobbs   PL14

	£		£
CPB	325.46		

P Taylor   PL21

	£		£
CPB	157.83		

S Dent   PL06

	£		£
CPB	163.58		

Test your understanding 4

Cashbook – Credit side

Date	Details	VAT £	Bank £
30 Nov	Motor expenses	40	240
30 Nov	Wages		6,200
30 Nov	Tax authorities		4,750

What will be the FOUR entries in the general ledger?

General ledger

Account name	Amount £	Debit/Credit
Motor expenses	200	Debit
VAT control account	40	Debit
Wages	6,200	Debit
VAT control account	4,750	Debit

Re-cap: Ledger accounts and the trial balance

Introduction

In this chapter we will be finding the correct ledger account balances by revising balancing ledger accounts as the basis for drafting an initial trial balance.

ASSESSMENT CRITERIA
Identify the purpose of the journal (2.3)
Produce journal entries to record accounting transactions (4.1)
Use journal entries to make adjustments in the ledger accounts (4.4)
Redraft the trial balance following adjustments (4.5)

CONTENTS

1   Balancing ledger accounts
2   Opening balances

1 Balancing ledger accounts

1.1 Introduction

The purpose of maintaining double entry ledger accounts is to provide information about the transactions and financial position of a business. Each type of transaction is gathered together and recorded in the appropriate ledger account, for example all sales are recorded in the sales account. Then at intervals it will be necessary to find the total of each of these types of transactions.

This is done by balancing each ledger account. This has been covered earlier in your studies but is worth revising here, by attempting Test your understanding 1.

Test your understanding 1

You are required to balance off the following ledger accounts:

Sales ledger control account

	£		£
SDB – invoices	5,426.23	CRB	3,226.56
		Discounts allowed	315.57

VAT account

	£		£
PDB	846.72	SDB	1,036.54

Sales account

	£		£
		SDB	2,667.45
		SDB	1,853.92

2 Opening balances

2.1 Introduction

If an account has a balance on it at the end of a period then it will have the same balance at the start of the next period. This is known as an opening balance.

A task in the assessment may involve journal entries to create opening balances. The key to this will be to identify whether the opening balance should be shown as a debit or a credit.

2.2 Debit or credit?

The key to determining whether an opening balance on a ledger account is a debit or a credit is to understand the general rules for debit and credit balances. This can be expressed in the assessment either as a journal, or by entering the amount directly onto the ledger account.

2.3 Debit and credit balance rules

The mnemonic DEAD/CLIC will help you determine if an entry should be made on the debit side or on the credit side of a ledger account.

Ledger account	
Debit:	**Credit:**
• **E**xpenses	• **L**iabilities
• **A**ssets	• **I**ncome
• **D**rawings	• **C**apital

🔆 Example 1

You are told that the opening balance on the sales ledger control account is £33,600, the opening balance on the purchases account is £115,200 and the opening balance on the purchases ledger control account is £12,700.

You are required to enter these into the relevant ledger accounts.

Solution

Sales ledger control account

	£		£
Balance brought down	33,600		

Purchases account

	£		£
Balance brought down	115,200		

Purchases ledger control account

	£		£
		Balance brought down	12,700

Assets and expenses normally have opening debit balances. Liabilities and income normally have opening credit balances.

2.4 Journals

A journal entry is a written instruction to the bookkeeping to enter a double entry into the general ledger accounts.

A journal can simply be the debit and credit that are required, but sometimes can include a description underneath to explain what the journal is doing.

The journal will be looked at further in chapter 4, but an outline of the journal needed to record opening balances is shown in the example below.

Example 2

Record the journal entries needed in the general ledger to account for the following balances.

Sales ledger control account	33,600
Purchases	115,200
Purchases ledger control account	12,700
Sales	138,240
Rent and rates	2,140

Solution

Sales ledger control account	33,600	Debit
Purchases	115,200	Debit
Purchases ledger control account	12,700	Credit
Sales	138,240	Credit
Rent and rates	2,140	Debit

To record the opening balances.

 Test your understanding 2

Would the balances on the following accounts be debit or credit balances?

(a) Sales account

(b) Discounts allowed account

(c) Discounts received account

(d) Wages expense account

 Test your understanding 3

The following are the opening balances for a new business. Complete the journal to record these balances.

Account name	Amount £	Debit/Credit
Bank overdraft	6,975	
Cash	275	
VAT payable	2,390	
Motor vehicles	10,500	
Plant and machinery	25,700	
Loan from bank	12,000	
Motor expenses	1,540	
Rent and rates	2,645	
Miscellaneous expenses	725	

Test your understanding 4

The following transactions all occurred on 1 December 20X1 and have been entered into the relevant books of prime entry (given below). However, no entries have yet been made into the ledger system. VAT has been calculated at a rate of 20%.

Purchases day book

Date	Details	Invoice no	Total	VAT	Purchases	Stationery
			£	£	£	£
20X1						
1 Dec	Bailey Limited	T151	240	40	200	
1 Dec	Byng & Company	10965	960	160	800	
1 Dec	Office Supplies Ltd	34565	336	56		280
1 Dec	O'Connell Frames	FL013	5,040	840	4,200	
	Totals		6,576	1,096	5,200	280

Purchases returns day book

Date	Details	Invoice no	Total	VAT	Purchases	Stationery
			£	£	£	
20X1						
1 Dec	O'Connell Frames	CO11	2,160	360	1,800	
1 Dec	Office Supplies Ltd	CR192	48	8		40
	Totals		2,208	368	1,800	40

Sales day book

Date	Details	Invoice no	Total	VAT	Sales
			£	£	£
20X1					
1 Dec	Bentley Brothers	H621	1,680	280	1,400
1 Dec	J & H Limited	H622	4,320	720	3,600
1 Dec	Furniture Galore	H623	4,800	800	4,000
1 Dec	The Sofa Shop	H624	2,640	440	2,200
	Totals		13,440	2,240	11,200

Opening balances

The following are some of the balances in the accounting records and are all relevant to you at the start of the day on 1 December 20X1:

	£
Credit suppliers	
Bailey Limited	11,750
Byng & Company	1,269
Office Supplies Limited	4,230
O'Connell Frames	423
PLCA	82,006
SLCA	180,312
Purchases	90,563
Sales	301,492
Purchases returns	306
Stationery	642
Discounts received	50
VAT (credit balance)	17,800

Receipts on 1 December 20X1

	Total £
Lili Chang (cash sale including VAT)	600
Bentley Brothers (credit customer)	5,875

Cheque issued

	Total £
Bailey Limited (in full settlement of debt of £819)	799

Task 1

Enter the opening balances listed above into the following accounts, blanks of which are provided on the following pages.

Task 2

Using the data shown above, enter all the relevant transactions into the accounts in the purchases ledger and general ledger. Entries to the sales ledger for receivables are not required.

Task 3

Enter the receipts and payments shown above into the cash book given on the following pages.

Task 4

Transfer any relevant sums from the cash book into the purchases ledger for payables and general ledger.

Task 5

Balance off all of the accounts and the cash book, showing clearly the balances carried down. The opening cash balance was £3,006. Find the closing balance on the cash book.

Tasks 1, 2, 4 and 5

Purchases ledger

Bailey Limited

	£		£

Byng & Company

	£		£

Office supplies Limited

	£		£

O'Connell Frames

	£		£

General ledger

PLCA

	£		£

SLCA

£		£

Purchases

£		£

Sales

£		£

Purchases returns

£		£

Stationery

£		£

Discounts received

£		£

VAT

£		£

Tasks 3, 4 and 5

Cash receipts book

Date	Narrative	Total £	VAT £	SLCA £	Cash sales £	Discount allowed £

Cash payments book

Date	Details	Cheque no	Code	Total £	VAT £	PLCA £	Cash purchases £	Other £	Discounts received £

Test your understanding 5

Complete the journal by showing whether each entry in the table would be a debit or credit:

Account name	Amount £	Dr ✓	Cr ✓
Cash	2,350		
Capital	20,360		
Motor vehicles	6,500		
Electricity	800		
Office expenses	560		
Loan from bank	15,000		
Cash at bank	6,400		
Factory equipment	14,230		
Rent	2,500		
Insurance	1,000		
Miscellaneous expenses	1,020		

Test your understanding 6

The following transactions took place on 16 February 2012 for Shedlands Ltd. These transactions should be entered into ledger accounts and balanced.

(a)   Cash of £20,000 was invested by the owner.

(b)   Some machinery costing £5,000 was purchased for use within the business. It was bought by cash.

(c)   A sale of £800 was made on credit.

(d)   A purchase of £320 was made on credit.

(e)   A sale of £450 was made on credit.

(f)   A receivable returned goods that cost £300 to Shedlands Ltd.

(g)   Shedlands paid a credit supplier £200.

(h)   A receipt of £500 was received from a receivable.

 Test your understanding 7

From Study text Test your understanding 6, extract a trial balance.

3   Summary

We started this chapter with a revision of balancing accounts and extended this to entering opening balances in the ledger accounts. These topics were all in Bookkeeping Transactions, but this is essential knowledge for Bookkeeping Controls. Double entries are a fundamental part of the assessment, so it is vital that you are happy with the concept of whether items are debit or credit balances. It is also essential that you are comfortable with balancing accounts.

Test your understanding answers

Test your understanding 1

Sales ledger control account

	£		£
SDB – invoices	5,426.23	CRB	3,226.56
		Discounts allowed	315.57
		Balance c/d	1,884.10
	5,426.23		5,426.23
Balance b/d	1,884.10		

VAT account

	£		£
PDB	846.72	SDB	1,036.54
Balance c/d	189.82		
	1,036.54		1,036.54
		Balance b/d	189.82

Sales account

	£		£
		SDB	2,667.45
Balance c/d	4,521.37	SDB	1,853.92
	4,521.37		4,521.37
		Balance b/d	4,521.37

Test your understanding 2

(a)   Credit balance

(b)   Debit balance

(c)   Credit balance

(d)   Debit balance

Test your understanding 3

Account name	Amount £	Debit/Credit
Bank overdraft	6,975	Credit
Cash	275	Debit
VAT payable	2,390	Credit
Motor vehicles	10,500	Debit
Plant and machinery	25,700	Debit
Loan from bank	12,000	Credit
Motor expenses	1,540	Debit
Rent and rates	2,645	Debit
Miscellaneous expenses	725	Debit

Test your understanding 4

Bailey Limited

		£			£
01 Dec	Bank	799	01 Dec	Balance b/d	11,750
01 Dec	Discount received	20	01 Dec	Purchases	240
01 Dec	Balance c/d	11,171			
		11,990			11,990
			02 Dec	Balance b/d	11,171

Byng & Company

		£			£
			01 Dec	Balance b/d	1,269
01 Dec	Balance c/d	2,229	01 Dec	Purchases	960
		2,229			2,229
			02 Dec	Balance b/d	2,229

Office Supplies Limited

		£			£
01 Dec	Purchases returns	48	01 Dec	Balance b/d	4,230
01 Dec	Balance c/d	4,518	01 Dec	Purchases	336
		4,566			4,566
			02 Dec	Balance b/d	4,518

O'Connell Frames

		£			£
01 Dec	Purchases returns	2,160	01 Dec	Balance b/d	423
01 Dec	Balance c/d	3,303	01 Dec	Purchases	5,040
		5,463			5,463
			02 Dec	Balance b/d	3,303

General ledger

PLCA

		£			£
01 Dec	Purchases returns	2,208	01 Dec	Balance b/d	82,006
01 Dec	Bank	799	01 Dec	Purchases	6,576
01 Dec	Discounts received	20			
01 Dec	Balance c/d	85,555			
		88,582			88,582
			02 Dec	Balance b/d	85,555

SLCA

		£			£
01 Dec	Balance b/d	180,312	01 Dec	Bank	5,875
01 Dec	Sales	13,440	01 Dec	Balance c/d	187,877
		193,752			193,752
02 Dec	Balance b/d	187,877			

Purchases

		£			£
01 Dec	Balance b/d	90,563			
01 Dec	PLCA	5,200	01 Dec	Balance c/d	95,763
		95,763			95,763
02 Dec	Balance b/d	95,763			

Sales

		£			£
			01 Dec	Balance b/d	301,492
			01 Dec	SLCA	11,200
01 Dec	Balance c/d	313,192	01 Dec	Bank	500
		313,192			313,192
			02 Dec	Balance b/d	313,192

Purchases returns

		£			£
			01 Dec	Balance b/d	306
01 Dec	Balance c/d	2,106	01 Dec	PLCA	1,800
		2,106			2,106
			02 Dec	Balance b/d	2,106

Stationery

		£			£
01 Dec	Balance b/d	642	01 Dec	PLCA	40
01 Dec	PLCA	280	01 Dec	Balance c/d	882
		922			922
02 Dec	Balance b/d	882			

Discounts received

		£			£
			01 Dec	Balance b/d	50
01 Dec	Balance c/d	70	01 Dec	Payables	20
		70			70
			02 Dec	Balance b/d	70

VAT

		£			£
01 Dec	PLCA	1,096	01 Dec	Balance b/d	17,800
			01 Dec	PLCA	368
			01 Dec	SLCA	2,240
01 Dec	Balance c/d	19,412	01 Dec	Bank	100
		20,508			20,508
			02 Dec	Balance b/d	19,412

Cash receipts book

Date	Narrative	Total £	VAT £	SLCA £	Other £	Discount £
20X1						
01 Dec	Lili Chang	600	100		500	
01 Dec	Benley Brothers	5,875		5,875		
		6,475	100	5,875	500	–

Cash payments book

Date	Details	Cheque no	Code	Total £	VAT £	PLCA £	Cash purchases £	Other £	Discounts received £
20X1 01 Dec	Bailey Ltd			799	–	799	–	–	20

	£
Opening balance	3,006
Add: Receipts	6,475
Less: Payments	(799)
Closing balance	8,682

Test your understanding 5

Account name	Amount £	Dr ✓	Cr ✓
Cash	2,350	✓	
Capital	20,360		✓
Motor vehicles	6,500	✓	
Electricity	800	✓	
Office expenses	560	✓	
Loan from bank	15,000		✓
Cash at bank	6,400	✓	
Factory equipment	14,230	✓	
Rent	2,500	✓	
Insurance	1,000	✓	
Miscellaneous expenses	1,020	✓	

Test your understanding 6

Bank

Date	Detail	£	Date	Detail	£
16.02	Capital	20,000	16.02	Machinery	5,000
16.02	SLCA	500	16.02	PLCA	200
				Balance c/d	15,300
		20,500			20,500
	Balance b/d	15,300			

Capital

Date	Detail	£	Date	Detail	£
			16.02	Bank	20,000
	Balance c/d	20,000			
		20,000			20,000
				Balance b/d	20,000

Machinery

Date	Detail	£	Date	Detail	£
16.02	Bank	5,000			
				Balance c/d	5,000
		5,000			5,000
	Balance b/d	5,000			

Sales

Date	Detail	£	Date	Detail	£
			16.02	SLCA	800
	Balance c/d	1,250	16.02	SLCA	450
		1,250			1,250
				Balance b/d	1,250

Purchases

Date	Detail	£	Date	Detail	£
16.02	PLCA	320			
				Balance c/d	320
		320			320
	Balance b/d	320			

PLCA

Date	Detail	£	Date	Detail	£
16.02	Bank	200	16.02	Purchases	320
	Balance c/d	120			
		320			320
				Balance b/d	120

Sales returns

Date	Detail	£	Date	Detail	£
16.02	SLCA	300			
				Balance c/d	300
		300			300
	Balance b/d	300			

SLCA

Date	Detail	£	Date	Detail	£
16.02	Sales	800		Sales returns	300
	Sales	450		Bank	500
				Balance c/d	450
		1,250			1,250
	Balance b/d	450			

Test your understanding 7

	£ Dr	£ Cr
Bank	15,300	
Capital		20,000
Machinery	5,000	
Sales		1,250
SLCA	450	
Purchases	320	
PLCA		120
Sales returns	300	
Total	**21,370**	**21,370**

Errors and suspense accounts

Introduction

When preparing a trial balance it may be necessary to open a suspense account to deal with any errors or omissions. The suspense account cannot be allowed to remain permanently in the trial balance, and must be cleared by correcting each of the errors that have caused the trial balance not to balance.

ASSESSMENT CRITERIA
Produce journal entries to correct errors not disclosed by the trial balance (4.2)
Produce journal entries to correct errors disclosed by the trial balance (4.3)

CONTENTS

1 The journal

1.1 Introduction

The journal is used to process double entries that are not obtained from the other books of prime entry, such as the sales day book. Journals will be used regularly within the assessment, so it is important to understand how these look and how to produce them.

Journals will either be used to process a new double entry, or to correct errors. The assessment will use journals for a variety of reasons, including opening balances (chapter 3), payroll transactions (chapter 6) and late adjustments such as irrecoverable debts and contras, which will be discussed in this section.

Journals are an essential part of the bookkeeping system, and are vital in performing adjustments to ensure that the financial statements are produced accurately.

When journals are required, they should be completed accurately and quickly to avoid delays to the accounts being processed. As always, any correspondence with other individuals within an organisation should be done in a courteous and professional manner.

This section will look at 2 common journals which were not seen within the Bookkeeping Transactions syllabus. These are irrecoverable debts and contras.

1.2 Irrecoverable debts

 Definition

An irrecoverable debt is a debt relating to a receivable which is not likely to be received; it is therefore not prudent for the business to consider this debt as an asset.

To prevent irrecoverable debts, it is important for the business to maintain an aged receivables ledger. This will ensure that the business is able to see which receivables are not paying on time.

Aged receivables ledgers are an extremely useful tool to the business. They will highlight balances which are overdue, but also customers who are regularly paying late. This will help the business become more efficient in collecting balances, which will in turn improve their cash flow.

1.3 Reasons for irrecoverable debts

A business may decide that a debt is irrecoverable (bad) for a number of reasons:

Customer is in liquidation – no cash will be received.

Customer is having difficulty paying although not officially in liquidation.

Customer disputes the debt and refuses to pay all or part of it.

1.4 Accounting for irrecoverable debts

The business must make an adjustment to write off the irrecoverable debt from the customer's account in the sales ledger and to write it off in the general ledger. The double entry in the general ledger is:

Dr   Irrecoverable debt expense

Cr   Sales ledger control account

Notice that the irrecoverable debt becomes an expense of the business, but is not deducted from sales. The sale was made in the anticipation of receiving the money but, if the debt is not to be received, this does not negate the sale it is just an added expense of the business.

The irrecoverable debt must also be written off in the individual receivable's account in the sales ledger by crediting the customer's account as this amount is not going to be received.

When you invoiced the customer you will have recorded the VAT and paid it to the tax authorities (HMRC). Once the debt is **more than 6 months old** and it has been determined that the customer is not going to pay you, you can reclaim that VAT back from the tax authorities.

Dr   Irrecoverable debt expense   Net amount

Dr   VAT control account   VAT amount

Cr   Sales ledger control account   Gross amount

1.5 Contra entries

A further type of adjustment that may be required to sales ledger and purchases ledger control accounts is a contra entry.

1.6 Why a contra entry is required

In some instances a business will be both a receivable and a payable of another business as it both buys from the business and sells to it. If this is the case then there will be money owed to the business and money owing from it. This can be simplified by making an adjustment known as a contra entry.

Example 1

James Associates has a customer, X Brothers. X Brothers also sells goods to James Associates. Therefore X Brothers is both a receivable and a payable of James Associates. The subsidiary ledger accounts of James Associates show the following position:

Sales ledger – receivables

X Brothers

	£		£
Balance b/d	250		

Purchases ledger – payables

X Brothers

	£		£
		Balance b/d	100

The problem here is that X Brothers owes James Associates £250 and is owed £100 by James Associates. If both parties are in agreement it makes more sense to net these two amounts off and to say that X Brothers owes James Associates just £150. This is achieved in accounting terms by a contra entry.

Solution

Step 1 Take the smaller of the two amounts and debit the purchases ledger account for the payable and credit the sales ledger account for the receivable with this amount.

Sales ledger – receivables

X Brothers

	£		£
Balance b/d	250	Contra	100

Purchases ledger – payables

X Brothers

	£		£
Contra	100	Balance b/d	100

Step 2 Balance off the accounts in the subsidiary ledgers.

Sales ledger – receivables

X Brothers

	£		£
Balance b/d	250	Contra	100
		Balance c/d	150
	———		———
	250		250
	———		———
Balance b/d	150		

Purchases ledger – payables

X Brothers

	£		£
Contra	100	Balance b/d	100
	———		———

This now shows that X Brothers owes £150 to James Associates and is owed nothing by James Associates.

Step 3 The double entry must also be carried out in the general ledger accounts. This is:

Dr   Purchases ledger control account

Cr   Sales ledger control account

When a contra entry is made you must remember not just to deal with the entries in the subsidiary ledgers but also to put through the double entry in the general ledger accounts, the sales ledger and purchases ledger control accounts.

2 Errors

2.1 Introduction

We saw in Processing Bookkeeping Transactions that one of the purposes of the trial balance is to provide a check on the accuracy of the double entry bookkeeping. If the trial balance does not balance then an error or a number of errors have occurred and this must be investigated and the errors corrected.

2.2 Errors detected by the trial balance

The following types of error will cause a difference in the trial balance and therefore will be detected by the trial balance and can be investigated and corrected:

A single entry – if only one side of a double entry has been made then this means that the trial balance will not balance e.g. if only the debit entry for receipts from receivables has been made then the debit total on the trial balance will exceed the credit balance.

A casting error – a casting error is where a list of items has been incorrectly totalled up, or a ledger balance has been balanced incorrectly. If this has only been applied to one balance, or to one side of the trial balance, this will mean that the trial balance will not balance.

A transposition error – if an amount in a ledger account or a balance on a ledger account has been transposed and incorrectly recorded then the trial balance will not balance e.g. a debit entry was recorded correctly as £5,276 but the related credit entry was entered as £5,726.

An extraction error – if a ledger account balance is incorrectly recorded on the trial balance either by recording the wrong figure or putting the balance on the wrong side of the trial balance then the trial balance will not balance.

An omission error – if a ledger account balance is inadvertently omitted from the trial balance then the trial balance will not balance.

Two entries on one side – instead of a debit and credit entry, if a transaction is entered as a debit in two accounts or as a credit in two accounts then the trial balance will not balance.

2.3 Errors not detected by the trial balance

A number of types of errors however will not cause the trial balance not to balance and therefore cannot be detected by preparing a trial balance:

An error of original entry – this is where the wrong figure is entered as both the debit and credit entry e.g. a payment of the electricity expense was correctly recorded as a debit in the electricity account and a credit to the bank account but it was recorded as £300 instead of £330.

A compensating error – this is where two separate errors are made, one on the debit side of the accounts and the other on the credit side, and by coincidence the two errors are of the same amount and therefore cancel each other out.

An error of omission – this is where an entire double entry is omitted from the ledger accounts. As both the debit and credit have been omitted the trial balance will still balance.

An error of commission – with this type of error a debit entry and an equal credit entry have been made but one of the entries has been to the wrong account e.g. if the electricity expense was debited to the rent account but the credit entry was correctly made in the bank account – here both the electricity account and rent account will be incorrect but the trial balance will still balance.

An error of principle – this is similar to an error of commission but the entry has been made in the wrong type of account e.g. if the electricity expense was debited to a non-current asset account – again both the electricity account and the non-current asset account would be incorrect but the trial balance would still balance.

It is important that a trial balance is prepared on a regular basis in order to check on the accuracy of the double entry. However not all errors in the accounting system can be found by preparing a trial balance.

2.4 Correction of errors

Errors will normally be corrected by putting through a journal. The procedure for correcting errors is as follows:

Step 1 – What has been done?

Determine the precise nature of the incorrect double entry that has been made.

Step 2 – What should have been done?

Determine the correct entries that should have been made.

Step 3 – What needs to be done to correct it?

Produce a journal entry that cancels the incorrect part and puts through the correct entries.

Example 2

The electricity expense of £450 has been correctly credited to the bank account but has been debited to the rent account.

Step 1 – What has been done?

The incorrect entry has been to debit the rent account with £450

Step 2 – What should have been done?

The correct entry is to debit the electricity account with £450

Step 3 – What needs to be done to correct it?

The journal entry required is:

Dr   Electricity account   £450

Cr   Rent account   £450

Note that this removes the incorrect debit from the rent account and puts the correct debit into the electricity account.

 Test your understanding 1

Colin returned some goods to a supplier because they were faulty. The original purchase price of these goods was £8,260.

The ledger clerk has correctly treated the double entry but used the figure £8,620.

What is the correcting entry which needs to be made?

3 Opening a suspense account

3.1   Introduction

A suspense account is used as a temporary account to deal with errors and omissions. It means that it is possible to continue with the production of financial accounts whilst the reasons for any errors are investigated and then corrected.

These will arise when the double entries made do not balance, either due to errors made or the bookkeeper only processing one side of the entry.

In the assessment, it is likely that you will have to deal with a suspense account. This can come in two main forms. You may be required to open up a suspense account in order to balance the trial balance, and then produce entries to clear the suspense account.

The method for clearing the suspense account is very similar to the steps outlined earlier for dealing with errors.

3.2 Reasons for opening a suspense account

A suspense account will be opened in two main circumstances:

(a) The bookkeeper does not know how to deal with one side of a transaction

(b) The trial balance does not balance.

3.3 Unknown entry

In some circumstances the bookkeeper may come across a transaction for which they are not certain of the correct double entry and therefore rather than making an error, one side of the entry will be put into a suspense account until the correct entry can be determined.

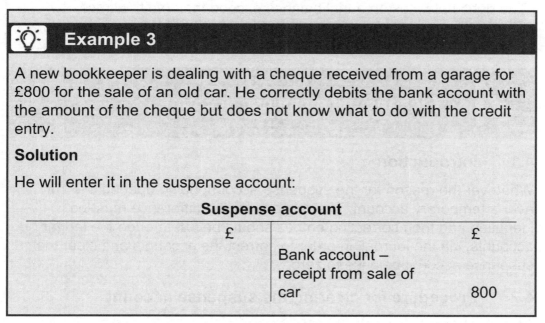

Example 3

A new bookkeeper is dealing with a cheque received from a garage for £800 for the sale of an old car. He correctly debits the bank account with the amount of the cheque but does not know what to do with the credit entry.

Solution

He will enter it in the suspense account:

Suspense account

	£		£
		Bank account – receipt from sale of car	800

3.4 Trial balance does not balance

If the total of the debits on the trial balance does not equal the total of the credits then an error or a number of errors have been made. These must be investigated, identified and eventually corrected. In the meantime the difference between the debit total and the credit total is inserted as a suspense account balance in order to make the two totals agree.

Example 4

The totals of the trial balance are as follows:

	Debits £	Credits £
Totals as initially extracted	108,367	109,444
Suspense account, to make the TB balance	1,077	
	109,444	109,444

Suspense

	£		£
Opening balance	1,077		

Test your understanding 2

The debit balances on a trial balance exceed the credit balances by £2,600. Open up a suspense account to record this difference.

4 Clearing the suspense account

4.1 Introduction

Whatever the reason for the suspense account being opened it is only ever a temporary account. The reasons for the difference must be identified and then correcting entries should be put through the ledger accounts, via the journal, in order to correct the accounts and clear the suspense account balance to zero.

4.2 Procedure for clearing the suspense account

Step 1 – What has been done?

Determine the incorrect entry that has been made or the omission from the ledger accounts.

Step 2 – What should have been done?

Work out what the correct entry should have been.

Step 3 – What needs to be done to correct it?

This is the tricky part. Some adjustments need to be made to the suspense account, and some will not. The key to this is step one. Remember that if the initial error made did not balance, a suspense account will have been created and now needs to be cleared.

If the initial error balanced, no suspense account would have been created and therefore no adjustment is required to clear the suspense account.

If there is an entry to be made in the suspense account put this into the suspense account – when all the corrections have been made the suspense account should normally have no remaining balance on it.

 Example 5

A trial balance has been extracted and did not balance. The debit column totalled £200,139 and the credit column totalled £200,239.

You discover that cash purchases of £100 have been correctly entered into the cash account but no entry has been made in the purchases account.

Draft a journal entry to correct this error, and complete the suspense ledger account.

Solution

Step 1 – What has been done?

Dr

    Cr Cash £100

As this does not balance, a **DEBIT** balance has been created on the suspense account of £100.

Suspense

Detail	Amount £	Detail	Amount £
TB	100		
	100		**100**

Step 2 – What should have been done?

The correct double entry should have been

Dr Purchases £100

    Cr Cash   £100

Step 3 – What needs to be done to correct it?

A debit entry is required in the purchases account and the credit is to the suspense account.

Dr Purchases   £100   (To record the purchase)

    Cr Suspense   £100   (To remove the suspense)

Being correction of double entry for cash purchases.

Suspense

Detail	Amount £	Detail	Amount £
TB	100	Journal 1 (detailed above)	100
	100		**100**

Remember that normally a journal entry needs a narrative to explain what it is for – however in some assessments you are told not to provide the narratives so always read the requirements carefully.

Example 6

On 31 December 20X0 the trial balance of John Jones failed to agree and the difference of £967 was entered as a debit balance on the suspense account. After the final accounts had been prepared the following errors were discovered and the difference was eliminated.

(1)   A purchase of goods from A Smith for £170 had been credited in error to the account of H Smith.

(2)   The purchases day book was undercast by £200.

(3)   Machinery purchased for £150 had been debited to the purchases account.

(4)   Discounts received of £130 had been posted to the debit of the discounts received account.

(5)   Rates paid by cheque £46 had been posted to the debit of the rates account as £64.

(6)   Cash drawings by the owner of £45 had been entered in the cash account correctly but not posted to the drawings account.

(7)   A non-current asset balance of £1,200 had been omitted from the trial balance.

Required:

(a)   Show the journal entries necessary to correct the above errors.

(b)   Show the entries in the suspense account to eliminate the differences entered in the suspense account.

Note: The control accounts are part of the double-entry.

Solution

(Note that not all the errors relate to the suspense account. Part of the way of dealing with these questions is to identify which entries do not relate to the suspense account. Do not assume that they all do just because this is a question about suspense accounts.)

Journal – John Jones

		Dr	Cr
	31 December 20X0	£	£
1	H Smith	170	
	A Smith		170
	Being adjustment of incorrect entry for purchases from A Smith – this correction takes place in the purchases ledger (no effect on suspense account)		
2	Purchases	200	
	Purchases ledger control account		200
	Being correction of undercast of purchases day book (no effect on suspense account as control account is the double entry. However the error should have been found during the reconciliation of the control account)		

3	Machinery	150	
	Purchases		150
	Being adjustment for wrong entry for machinery purchased (no effect on suspense account)		
4	Suspense account	260	
	Discount received		260
	Being correction of discounts entered on wrong side of account		
5	Suspense account	18	
	Rates		18
	Being correction of transposition error to rates account		
6	Drawings	45	
	Suspense account		45
	Being completion of double entry for drawings		
7	Non-current asset	1,200	
	Suspense account		1,200
	Being inclusion of non-current asset balance. There is no double entry for this error in the ledger as the mistake was to omit the item from the trial balance		

Suspense account

	£		£
Difference in trial balance	967	Drawings	45
Discounts received	260	Non-current asset per trial balance	1,200
Rates	18		
	1,245		1,245

Make sure you realise that not all error corrections will require any entry to the suspense account.

Test your understanding 3

GA extracted the following trial balance from his ledgers at 31 May 20X4.

	£	£
Petty cash	20	
Capital		1,596
Drawings	1,400	
Sales		20,607
Purchases	15,486	
Purchases returns		210
Inventory (1 January 20X4)	2,107	
Fixtures and fittings	710	
Sales ledger control	1,819	
Purchases ledger control		2,078
Carriage on purchases	109	
Carriage on sales	184	
Rent and rates	460	
Light and heat	75	
Postage and telephone	91	
Sundry expenses	190	
Cash at bank	1,804	
	24,455	24,491

The trial balance did not agree. On investigation, GA discovered the following errors which had occurred during the month of May.

(1) In extracting the receivables balance the **credit** side of the sales ledger control account had been overcast by £10.

(2) An amount of £4 for carriage on sales had been posted in error to the carriage on purchases account.

(3) A credit note for £17 received from a payable had been entered in the purchase returns account but no entry had been made in the purchases ledger control account.

(4) £35 charged by Builders Ltd for repairs to GA's private residence had been charged, in error, to the sundry expenses account.

(5) A payment of a telephone bill of £21 had been entered correctly in the cash book but had been posted, in error, to the postage and telephone account as £12.

Required:

(a) Create a suspense account to balance the trial balance.

(b) State what corrections you would make in GA's ledger accounts (using journal entries) and re-write the trial balance as it should appear after all the above corrections have been made. Show how the suspense account is cleared.

5 Re-drafting the trial balance

Once the suspense account has been cleared, it is important to re-draft the trial balance to ensure that the debit column and credit column agree.

 Example 7

On 30 November an initial trial balance was extracted which did not balance, and a suspense account was opened. On 1 December journal entries were prepared to correct the errors that had been found, and clear the suspense account. The list of balances and the journal entries are shown below.

Re-draft the trial balance by placing the figures in the debit or credit column, after taking into account the journal entries which will clear suspense.

	Balances as at 30 November	Balances as at 1 December	
		Debit £	Credit £
Motor vehicles	10,500		
Inventory	2,497		
Bank overdraft	1,495		
Petty cash	162		
Sales ledger control	6,811		
Purchases ledger control	2,104		
VAT owing to tax authorities	1,329		
Capital	15,000		
Sales	47,036		
Purchases	27,914		
Purchase returns	558		
Wages	12,000		
Motor expenses	947		
Drawings	6,200		
Suspense (debit balance)	491		

Journals

Account	Debit £	Credit £
Motor expenses		9
Suspense	9	
Being to correct transposition error when recording expense		

Account	Debit £	Credit £
Drawings	500	
Suspense		500
Being to correctly analyse unknown cheque payment		

Solution

	Balances as at 30 November	Balances as at 1 December	
		Debit £	Credit £
Motor vehicles	10,500	10,500	
Inventory	2,497	2,497	
Bank overdraft	1,495		1,495
Petty cash	162	162	
Sales ledger control	6,811	6,811	
Purchases ledger control	2,104		2,104
VAT owing to tax authorities	1,329		1,329
Capital	15,000		15,000
Sales	47,036		47,036
Purchases	27,914	27,914	
Purchase returns	558		558
Wages	12,000	12,000	
Motor expenses	947	**938**	
Drawings	6,200	**6,700**	
Suspense (debit balance)	491		
		67,522	**67,522**

The drawings and the motor expenses figures have been amended for the journals and the trial balance columns agree without the need for a suspense account.

Test your understanding 4

Which of the errors below are, or are not, disclosed by the trial balance? (Ignore VAT in all cases)

(a) Recording a receipt from a receivable in the bank account only.

(b) Recording bank payment of £56 for motor expenses as £65 in the expense account.

(c) Recording a credit purchase on the debit side of the purchase ledger control account and the credit side of the purchases account.

(d) Recording a payment for electricity in the insurance account.

(e) Recording a bank receipt for cash sales on the credit side of both the bank and the sales account.

(f) Incorrectly calculating the balance on the motor vehicles account.

(g) Writing off an irrecoverable debt in the irrecoverable debt expense and sales ledger control accounts only.

(h) An account with a ledger balance of £3,500 was recorded on the Trial Balance as £350.

Test your understanding 5

Luxury Caravans Ltd's initial trial balance includes a suspense account with a balance of £2,800 as shown below:

	£
Receivables	33,440
Bank (debit balance)	2,800
Sales	401,300
Inventory	24,300
Wages	88,400
Telephone	2,200
Motor car	12,000
VAT (credit balance)	5,300
Electricity	3,800
Rent	16,200
Purchases	241,180
Purchases returns	1,600
Sales returns	4,200
Office equipment	5,000
Capital	49,160
Motor expenses	5,040
Discounts allowed	4,010
Discounts received	2,410
Payables	20,000
Drawings	40,000
Suspense (credit balance)	2,800

The following errors have been discovered:

- Rent of £200 has been debited to the motor expenses account.

- An electricity payment of £800 has been debited to both the electricity and the bank account.

- The balance on the discounts received account has been incorrectly extracted to the TB – the actual balance on the ledger account was £4,210.

- The balance on the miscellaneous expenses account of £500 was omitted from the TB.

- The purchase returns day book for 22 May was incorrectly totalled, as shown below:

Purchase returns day book					
Date	Details	Credit note number	Total £	VAT £	Net £
22 May	Todd Ltd	578	120	20	100
22 May	Fallon Ltd	579	96	16	80
22 May	Dean's plc	580	144	24	120
	Totals		360	160	300

Required:

(a) Produce journal entries to correct all of the errors above.

(b) Re-draft the trial balance using the balances above and your journal entries to show the suspense account has been cleared.

6 Summary

Preparation of the trial balance is an important element of control over the double entry system but it will not detect all errors. The trial balance will still balance if a number of types of error are made. If the trial balance does not balance then a suspense account will be opened temporarily to make the debits equal the credits in the trial balance. The errors or omissions that have caused the difference on the trial balance must be discovered and then corrected using journal entries. Not all errors will require an entry to the suspense account. However, any that do should be put through the suspense account in order to try to eliminate the balance on the account.

Test your understanding answers

 Test your understanding 1

Step 1

The purchases ledger control account has been debited and the purchases returns account credited but with £8,620 rather than £8,260.

Step 2

Both of the entries need to be reduced by the difference between the amount used and the correct amount (8,620 – 8,260) = £360.

Step 3

Journal entry:	£	£
Dr Purchases returns account	360	
Cr Purchases ledger control account		360

Being correction of misposting of purchases returns.

 Test your understanding 2

As the debit balances exceed the credit balances the balance needed is a credit balance to make the two totals equal.

Suspense account

	£		£
		Opening balance	2,600

Test your understanding 3

(a) A suspense account will be opened with a DEBIT balance of £36, as the credit side of the TB is £36 larger than the debit side.

(b) See below.

What has been done?	What should have been done?	What should be done to correct it?
The credit side has been overcast, meaning that the receivable balance is UNDERSTATED by £10. Dr Suspense £10 Cr Receivables £10	Receivables should have been totalled to £1,829 rather than £1,819.	Dr Receivables £10 Cr Suspense £10
Dr Carriage on purchases £4 Cr Cash £4	Dr Carriage on sales £4 Cr Cash £4	Dr Carriage on sales £4 Cr Carriage on purchases £4
Dr Suspense £17 Cr Purchase returns £17	Dr PLCA £17 Cr Purchase returns £17	Dr PLCA £17 Cr Suspense £17
Dr Sundry expenses £35 Cr Cash £35	Dr Drawings £35 Cr Cash £35	Dr Drawings £35 Cr Sundry expenses £35
Dr Phone expense £12 Cr Cash £21 Dr Suspense £9	Dr Phone expense £21 Cr Cash £21	Dr Phone expense 9 Cr Suspense 9

			Dr £	Cr £
1	Debit	Sales ledger control account	10	
	Credit	Suspense account		10
	correction of undercast in sales ledger control account			
2	Debit	Carriage on sales	4	
	Credit	Carriage on purchases		4
	being correction of wrong posting			
3	Debit	Purchases ledger control account	17	
	Credit	Suspense account		17
	being correction of omitted entry			
4	Debit	Drawings	35	
	Credit	Sundry expenses		35
	being payment for private expenses			
5	Debit	Postage and telephone	9	
	Credit	Suspense account		9
	being correction of transposition error			

Suspense account

	£		£
Difference per trial balance (24,455 – 24,491)	36	SLCA	10
		PLCA	17
		Postage and telephone	9
	36		36

Trial balance after adjustments

	Dr £	Cr £
Petty cash	20	
Capital		1,596
Drawings	1,435	
Sales		20,607
Purchases	15,486	
Purchases returns		210
Inventory at 1 January 20X4	2,107	
Fixtures and fittings	710	
Sales ledger control account	1,829	
Purchases ledger control account		2,061
Carriage on purchases	105	
Carriage on sales	188	
Rent and rates	460	
Light and heat	75	
Postage and telephone	100	
Sundry expenses	155	
Cash at bank	1,804	
	24,474	24,474

Test your understanding 4

(a)   Error disclosed by the trial balance – a single entry

(b)   Error disclosed by the trial balance – a transposition error

(c)   Error NOT disclosed by the trial balance – a reversal of entries

(d)   Error NOT disclosed by the trial balance – an error of commission

(e)   Error disclosed by the trial balance – two entries on one side

(f)   Error disclosed by the trial balance – a casting error

(g)   Error NOT disclosed by the trial balance – double entry is correct, it is only the subsidiary sales ledger that hasn't been updated

(h)   Error disclosed by the trial balance – an extraction error

Test your understanding 5

Account name	Amount £	Dr ✓	Cr ✓
Rent	200	✓	
Motor expenses	200		✓

Account name	Amount £	Dr ✓	Cr ✓
Bank	1,600		✓
Suspense	1,600	✓	

Account name	Amount £	Dr ✓	Cr ✓
Discounts received	1,800		✓
Suspense	1,800	✓	

Account name	Amount £	Dr ✓	Cr ✓
Miscellaneous expenses	500	✓	
Suspense	500		✓

Account name	Amount £	Dr	Cr
VAT	100	✓	
Suspense	100		✓

Re-drafted trial balance

	£	£
Receivables	33,440	
Bank	1,200	
Sales		401,300
Inventory	24,300	
Wages	88,400	
Telephone	2,200	
Motor car	12,000	
VAT		5,200
Electricity	3,800	
Rent	16,400	
Purchases	241,180	
Purchases returns		1,600
Sales returns	4,200	
Office equipment	5,000	
Capital		49,160
Motor expenses	4,840	
Discounts allowed	4,010	
Discounts received		4,210
Payables		20,000
Drawings	40,000	
Miscellaneous expenses	500	
	481,470	481,470

Control accounts and reconciliations

5

Introduction

In this chapter we will consider three key control accounts; the sales ledger control account, purchase ledger control account and the VAT control account.

The sales and purchase ledger control accounts will then be reconciled to the list of individual account balances in the subsidiary ledgers.

Finally, the VAT control account will be examined, finishing with verifying whether the closing balance is a liability to the tax authorities or an amount receivable from them.

ASSESSMENT CRITERIA	CONTENTS
Identify the purpose of control accounts (2.1)	1 Accounting for receivables
Identify the purpose of reconciliation (2.2)	2 Sales ledger control account reconciliation
Produce control accounts (3.1)	3 Accounting for payables
Reconcile control accounts (3.2)	4 Purchases ledger control account reconciliation
	5 Cause of the difference
	6 The VAT control account

1 Accounting for receivables

1.1 Introduction

Within the general ledger the total amount outstanding from receivables is shown in the sales ledger control account. The sales ledger control account may also be referred to as the receivables ledger control account.

The totals of credit sales (from the sales day book), returns from customers (from the sales returns day book), cash received (from the analysed cash book) and discounts allowed (from the discounts allowed daybook) are posted to this account. This account therefore shows the total receivables outstanding. It does not give details about individual customers' balances. This is available in the sales ledger for receivables.

However, as both records are compiled from the same sources, the total balances on the customers' individual accounts should equal the outstanding balance on the control account at any time.

1.2 Double entry system

The double entry system operates as follows.

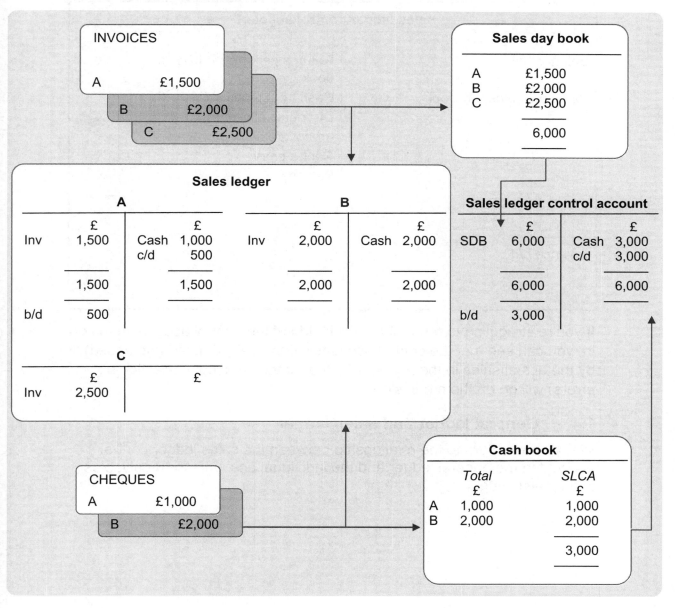

Notice that the remaining balance on the control account (£3,000) is equal to the sum of the remaining balances on the individual receivables' accounts (A £500 + C £2,500).

If all of the accounting entries have been made correctly then the balance on the sales ledger control account should equal the total of the balances on each of the individual receivables' accounts in the sales ledger.

1.3 Proforma sales ledger control account

A sales ledger control account normally appears like this.

Sales ledger control account			
	£		£
Balance b/d	X	Returns per sales returns day book	X
Sales per sales day book	X	Cash from receivables	X
		Discounts allowed	X
		Irrecoverable debt written off	X
		Contra entry	X
		Balance c/d	X
	X		X
Balance b/d			

If you're struggling to remember which side of the control account items go in, you can see that the control account is only really debited (increased) by the actual sales in the period. All other entries (except correction of errors) will go on the credit side.

1.4 General ledger and sales ledger

We will now return to the relationship between the sales ledger control account in the general ledger and the individual accounts for receivables in the sales ledger.

Example 1

James has been trading for two months. He has four credit customers. James is not registered for VAT. Here is the day book for the first two months:

Sales day book (SDB)

Date	Customer	Invoice	£
02.2.X4	Peter Brown	01	50.20
05.2.X4	Ian Smith	02	80.91
07.2.X4	Sid Parsons	03	73.86
23.2.X4	Eva Lane	04	42.30
	Total		247.27
09.3.X4	Ian Smith	05	23.96
15.3.X4	Sid Parsons	06	34.72
20.3.X4	Peter Brown	07	12.60
24.3.X4	Sid Parsons	08	93.25
31.3.X4	Total		164.53

Here is the receipts side of the analysed cash book for March 20X4 (no cash was received from receivables in February).

Cash receipts book (CRB)

Date	Narrative	Total £	Cash sales £	Sales ledger £	Rent £
01.3.X4	Peter Brown	50.20		50.20	
03.3.X4	Clare Jones	63.80	63.80		
04.3.X4	Molly Dell	110.00			110.00
12.3.X4	Sid Parsons	50.00		50.00	
13.3.X4	Emily Boyd	89.33	89.33		
20.3.X4	Frank Field	92.68	92.68		
25.3.X4	Eva Lane	42.30		42.30	
31.3.X4	Total	498.31	245.81	142.50	110.00

We will write up the sales ledger and the sales ledger control account and compare the balances.

Solution

Sales ledger – receivables

Peter Brown

		£			£
02.2.X4	01	50.20	28.2.X4	Balance c/d	50.20
		50.20			50.20
01.3.X4	Balance b/d	50.20	01.3.X4	Cash	50.20
20.3.X4	07	12.60	31.3.X4	Balance c/d	12.60
		62.80			62.80
01.4.X4	Balance b/d	12.60			

Eva Lane

		£			£
23.2.X4	04	42.30	28.2.X4	Balance c/d	42.30
		42.30			42.30
01.3.X4	Balance b/d	42.30	25.3.X4	Cash	42.30

Sid Parsons

		£			£
07.2.X4	03	73.86	28.2.X4	Balance c/d	73.86
		73.86			73.86
01.3.X4	Balance b/d	73.86	12.3.X4	Cash	50.00
15.3.X4	06	34.72	31.3.X4	Balance c/d	151.83
24 3 X4	08	93.25			
		201.83			201.83
01.4.X4	Balance b/d	151.83			

Ian Smith

		£			£
05.2.X4	02	80.91	28.2.X4	Balance c/d	80.91
		80.91			80.91
01.3.X4	Balance b/d	80.91	31.3.X4	Balance c/d	104.87
09.3.X4	05	23.96			
		104.87			104.87
01.4.X4	Balance b/d	104.87			

Sales ledger control account

		£			£
28.2.X4	SDB	247.27	28.2.X4	Balance c/d	247.27
		247.27			247.27
01.3.X4	Balance b/d	247.27	31.3.X4	CRB	142.50
31.3.X4	SDB	164.53	31.3.X4	Balance c/d	269.30
		411.80			411.80
01.4.X4	Balance b/d	269.30			

Let us compare balances at 31 March 20X4.

Subsidiary ledger – receivables

	£
Peter Brown	12.60
Eva Lane	–
Sid Parsons	151.83
Ian Smith	104.87
	269.30
Sales ledger control account	269.30

As the double entry has been correctly carried out, the total of the balances on the individual receivables' accounts in the sales ledger is equal to the balance on the sales ledger control account.

2 Sales ledger control account reconciliation

2.1 Introduction

Comparing the sales ledger control account balance with the total of the sales ledger accounts is a form of internal control. The reconciliation should be performed on a regular basis by the sales ledger clerk and reviewed and approved by an independent person.

If the total of the balances on the sales ledger do not equal the balance on the sales ledger control account then an error or errors have been made in either the general ledger or sales ledger, and these must be discovered and corrected.

2.2 Journal entries

We saw earlier how a journal can be used to enter opening balances to start a new period of accounts. Journal entries are also used for unusual items that do not appear in the primary records, or for the correction of errors or making of adjustments to ledger accounts.

A typical journal entry to write off an irrecoverable debt is shown below:

Sequential journal number

Authorisation

Description of why double entry is necessary

Double entry

JOURNAL ENTRY		No: 06671		
Prepared by:	P Freer			
Authorised by:	P Simms			
Date:	3 October 20X2			
Narrative:				
To write off irrecoverable debt from L C Hamper				
Account		*Code*	*Debit*	*Credit*
Irrecoverable debts expense		ML28	102.00	
Receivables' control		ML06		102.00
TOTALS			102.00	102.000

Equal totals as journal must balance

Example 2

The total sales for the month were posted from the sales day book as £4,657.98 instead of £4,677.98. This must be corrected using a journal entry.

Solution

The journal entry to correct this error will be as follows:

JOURNAL ENTRY		No: 97		
Prepared by:	A Graimm			
Authorised by:	L R Ridinghood			
Date:	23.7.X3			
Narrative:				
To correct error in posting from SDB				
Account		*Code*	*Debit*	*Credit*
Sales ledger control		ML11	20	
Sales		ML56		20
TOTALS			20	20

The adjustment required is to increase receivables and sales by £20 therefore a debit to sales ledger control and a credit to sales is needed.

2.3 Adjustments in the subsidiary ledger

Adjustments in the subsidiary ledger do not need to be shown in a journal entry. Journal entries are only required for adjustments to the general ledger.

These adjustments should be recorded in memorandum form, with proper authorisation.

2.4 Procedure for a sales ledger control account reconciliation

(1) The balances on the sales ledger accounts for receivables are extracted, listed and totalled.

(2) The sales ledger control account is balanced.

(3) If the two figures differ, then the reasons for the difference must be investigated.

Reasons may include the following:

- an error in the casting of the day book (the total is posted to the control account whereas the individual invoices are posted to the individual accounts and, therefore, if the total is incorrect, a difference will arise)

- a transposition error (the figures are switched around, e.g. £87 posted as £78) which could be made in posting either:

    (a) to the control account (the total figure); or

    (b) to the individual accounts (the individual transactions)

- a casting error in the cash book column relating to the control account (the total is posted)

- a balance omitted from the list of individual accounts

- a credit balance on an individual account in the sales ledger for receivables which has automatically and wrongly been assumed to be a debit balance.

(4) Differences which are errors in the control account should be corrected in the control account.

(5) Differences which are errors in the individual accounts should be corrected by adjusting the list of balances and, of course, the account concerned.

Test your understanding 1

Would the following errors cause a difference to occur between the balance of the sales ledger control account and the total of the balances in the sales ledger?

(a) The total column of the sales day book was overcast by £100.

(b) In error H Lambert's account in the sales ledger was debited with £175 instead of M Lambert's account.

(c) An invoice for £76 was recorded in the sales day book as £67.

Example 3

The balance on the sales ledger control account for a business at 31 March 20X3 is £14,378.37. The total of the list of sales ledger balances for receivables is £13,935.37.

The difference has been investigated and the following errors have been identified:

- the sales day book was overcast by £1,000

- a credit note for £150 was entered into an individual receivable's account as an invoice

- discounts allowed of £143 were correctly accounted for in the sales ledger but were not entered into the general ledger accounts

- a credit balance on one receivable's account of £200 was mistakenly listed as a debit balance when totalling the individual receivable accounts in the sales ledger.

Prepare the reconciliation between the balance on the sales ledger control account and the total of the individual balances on the sales ledger accounts.

Solution

Step 1   Amend the sales ledger control account for any errors that have been made.

Sales ledger control account

	£		£
Balance b/d	14,378.37	SDB overcast	1,000.00
		Discounts allowed	143.00
		Balance c/d	13,235.37
	14,378.37		14,378.37
Balance b/d	13,235.37		

Step 2 Correct the total of the list of balances in the sales ledger.

	£
Original total	13,935.37
Less: Credit note entered as invoice (2 × 150)	(300.00)
Credit balance entered as debit balance (2 × 200)	(400.00)
	13,235.37

 Test your understanding 2

The balance on Diana's sales ledger control account at 31 December 20X6 was £15,450. The balances on the individual accounts in the sales ledger have been extracted and total £15,705. On investigation the following errors are discovered:

(a) a debit balance of £65 has been omitted from the list of balances

(b) discounts totalling £70 have been recorded in the individual accounts but not in the control account

(c) the sales day book was 'overcast' by £200

(d) a contra entry for £40 has not been entered into the control account, and

(e) an invoice for £180 was recorded correctly in the sales day book but was posted to the receivables' individual account as £810.

Prepare the sales ledger control account reconciliation.

Test your understanding 3

The balance on the sales ledger control account for a business at 30 June 2012 is £18,971.12. The total of the list of subsidiary ledger balances for receivables is £21,761.12. The difference has been investigated and the following errors have been identified:

(a)   The sales day book was undercast by £1,500.

(b)   An invoice for £300 was entered twice into the subsidiary sales ledger.

(c)   Discounts allowed of £143 were entered in the sales ledger control account as £133. They were correctly entered in the subsidiary sales ledger.

(d)   A credit note for £1,000 was omitted from one receivable's account, although it was correctly entered in the general ledger.

Correct any errors in the sales ledger control account and prepare the reconciliation between the balance on that account and the total of the individual balances on the subsidiary ledger accounts.

3 Accounting for payables

3.1   Introduction

As we have previously seen, the total amount payable to payables is recorded in the general ledger in the purchases ledger control account. This may also be referred to as the payables ledger control account. The total of credit purchases from the purchases day book, returns to suppliers from the purchases returns day book, the total payments to payables from the cash payments book and discounts received taken from the discounts received daybook are all posted to this account.

The purchases ledger control account shows the total amount that is payable to payables but it does not show the amount owed to individual suppliers. This information is provided by the purchases ledger which contains an account for each individual payable.

Each individual invoice from the purchases day book and each individual credit note from the purchases returns day book is posted to the relevant payable's account in the purchases ledger. Similarly each individual payment to payables and discounts received are posted from the cash payments book to the individual payables' accounts in the purchases ledger.

3.2 Relationship between the purchases ledger control account and the balances in the purchases ledger

The information that is being posted to the purchases ledger control account in total and to the individual accounts in the purchases ledger as individual entries are from the same sources and should in total be the same figures.

Therefore, just as with the sales ledger control account, if the double entry and entries to the purchases ledger have been correctly carried out then the balance on the purchases ledger control account should be equal to the total of the list of balances on the individual payables' accounts in the purchases ledger.

3.3 Proforma purchases ledger control account

A purchases ledger control account normally appears like this.

Purchases ledger control account			
	£		£
Payments to suppliers per analysed cash book		Balance b/d	X
Cash	X	Purchases per purchases day book	X
Discount received	X		
Returns per purchases returns day book	X		
Contra entry	X		
Balance c/d	X		
	X		X
		Balance b/d	X

If all of the accounting entries have been correctly made then the balance on this purchases ledger control account should equal the total of the balances on the individual supplier accounts in the purchases ledger.

4 Purchases ledger control account reconciliation

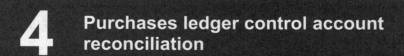

4.1 Introduction

At each month end the purchases ledger clerk must reconcile the purchases ledger control account and the purchases ledger, just as the sales ledger clerk performed the sales ledger control account reconciliation.

Remember that as well as investigating and discovering the differences, the control account and the individual accounts in the purchases ledger must also be amended for any errors.

4.2 Adjustments to the purchases ledger control account

Any corrections or adjustments made to the purchases ledger control account can be documented as a journal entry.

 Example 4

The total purchases for the month were posted from the purchases day book as £2,547.98 instead of £2,457.98. Prepare a journal to correct this error.

Solution

The journal entry to correct this error will be as follows:

JOURNAL ENTRY		No: 253		
Prepared by:	P Charming			
Authorised by:	U Sister			
Date:	29.8.X5			
Narrative:				
To correct error in posting to payables' control account				
Account		*Code*	*Debit*	*Credit*
Purchase ledger control		GL56	90	
Purchases		GL34		90
TOTALS			90	90

In this case both PLCA and purchases need to be reduced by £90. Therefore a debit to the purchases ledger control and a credit to purchases are required.

4.3 Adjustments in the purchases ledger

Adjustments in the purchases ledger do not need to be documented in a journal entry. Journal entries are only required for adjustments to the general ledger.

Example 5

The balance on the purchases ledger control account for a business at 30 June was £12,159. The total of the balances on the individual payables' accounts in the purchases ledger was £19,200.

The following errors were also found:

- the cash payments book had been undercast by £20

- an invoice from Thomas Ltd, a credit supplier, for £2,400 was correctly entered in the purchases ledger but had been missed out of the addition of the total in the purchases day book

- an invoice from Fred Singleton for £2,000 plus VAT was included in his individual account in the purchases ledger at the net amount

- an invoice from Horace Shades for £6,000 was entered into the individual account in the purchases ledger twice

- the same invoice is for £6,000 plus sales tax but the VAT had not been included in the purchases ledger

- returns to Horace Shades of £261 had been omitted from the purchases ledger.

You are required to reconcile the purchases ledger control account with the balances on the purchases ledger accounts at 30 June.

Solution

Step 1 Amend the purchases ledger control account to show the correct balance.

Purchases ledger control account

	£		£
Undercast of CPB	20	Balance b/d	12,159
Balance c/d	14,539	Invoice omitted from PDB	2,400
	_____		_____
	14,559		14,559
	_____		_____
		Amended balance b/d	14,539

Step 2   Correct the total of the list of purchases ledger balances.

	£
Original total	19,200
Add: Fred Singleton VAT	400
Less: Horace Shades invoice included twice	(6,000)
Add: Horace Shades VAT	1,200
Less: Horace Shades returns	(261)
Amended total of list of balances	14,539

Remember that invoices from suppliers should be included in the individual suppliers' accounts in the purchases ledger at the gross amount, including VAT.

 Test your understanding 4

How would each of the following be dealt with in the purchases ledger control account reconciliation?

(a)   A purchase invoice for £36 from P Swift was credited to P Short's account in the subsidiary ledger.

(b)   A purchase invoice for £96 not entered in the purchases day book.

(c)   An undercast of £20 in the total column of the purchases day book.

(d)   A purchase invoice from Short & Long for £42 entered as £24 in the purchases day book.

5   Cause of the difference

You may sometimes be asked you to say what has caused the difference between the control account and the list of balances. If you are asked to do this, the difference will usually be caused by just one error.

An example will illustrate this.

Example 6

XYZ Ltd has made the following entries in the sales ledger control account.

	£
Opening balance 1 April 20X7	49,139
Credit sales posted from the sales day book	35,000
Discounts allowed	328
Irrecoverable debt written off	127
Cash received from receivables	52,359

The list of balances from the sales ledger totals £31,579.

(a) Calculate the closing balance on the SLCA at 31 April 2007.

(b) State one reason for the difference between the SLCA balance and the total of the list of balances.

Solution

(a) The SLCA

Sales ledger control account

	£		£
Balance b/d	49,139	Discount allowed	328
SDB – sales	35,000	Irrecoverable debt	127
		Cash received	52,359
		Balance c/d	31,325
	–––––		–––––
	84,139		84,139
	–––––		–––––

(b)	Total of sales ledger balances	31,579
	Balance of SLCA at 30 April 20X7	31,325
		–––––
	Difference	254
		–––––

Note

You have to look for the fairly obvious clues and also make some assumptions

(i) It's reasonable to assume that the control account is correct – it may not be, so be careful.

(ii) Calculate the difference and determine whether the list total is larger than the SLCA balance or vice versa.

(iii) See if one of the figures given in the question is the same as the difference or double the difference.

If a figure given is the same as the difference then it is likely that a number has been left out of an account.

If a figure given is double the difference then it is likely that a number has been entered on the wrong side of an account, or possibly entered twice.

- In the above question, the difference is £254.

- The total of the list of ledger balances is bigger than the SLCA balance.

- £254 is not a figure given in the question but the amount £127 is given and the difference is twice this figure.

One possible reason for this is that the irrecoverable debt write off (£127) was entered on the debit side of a ledger account in the sales ledger – that would have made the total of the list £254 larger. Of course there are a million possible reasons – perhaps there was an invoice for £254 and it was entered twice in a sales ledger account – that would have caused the difference, but the assessor is looking for something obvious in the figures given to you – not some speculative reason.

 Test your understanding 5

Show whether each entry will be a debit or credit in the sales ledger control account in the general ledger:

TRANSACTION	Amount (£)	DEBIT ✓	CREDIT ✓
Balance brought down	60,980		
Goods sold on credit	12,566		
Returns made by credit customers	4,224		
Payments made by credit customers	15,789		
Discounts allowed	569		
Irrecoverable debt written off	872		

What will the balance brought down be?

The following balances were identified in the subsidiary ledgers:

COMPANY	£
ABC Ltd	14,600 Dr
Shoebox Ltd	7,860 Dr
Heels R Us	12,500 Dr
Feet First Ltd	10,043 Dr
Twinkle Toes plc	7,961 Dr

Reconcile the balance per the control account to the balance per the subsidiary ledgers.

Balance per control account:

Balance per subsidiary ledgers:

Difference:

What may have caused the difference between the control account and the subsidiary ledgers?

(a)   Discounts allowed may have been omitted from the subsidiary ledger.

(b)   Discounts allowed may have been omitted from the control account.

(c)   Irrecoverable debts may have been omitted from the subsidiary ledger.

(d)   Irrecoverable debts may have been omitted from the control account.

6   The VAT control account

Within Bookkeeping Transactions we learned about the operation of VAT to enable us to calculate the amount we would charge on our sales, and the amounts we would reclaim on our purchases. We now need to consider how these transactions would look within the third control account within the general ledger, the VAT control account, and to appreciate that it is the difference between these two amounts that must be paid to or received from the tax authorities (HMRC).

In the assessment, students must be able to process the entries in addition to verifying whether the balance represents a liability to HMRC or an asset from them.

Example 7

The following VAT figures have been extracted from your day books. Complete the VAT control account, and find the balance.

Sales day book	22,436
Sales returns day book	674
Purchases day book	15,327

Solution

VAT account

Details	Amount £	Details	Amount £
Sales returns (SRDB)	674	Sales (SDB)	22,436
Purchases (PDB)	15,327		
Balance c/d	6,435		
	22,436		**22,436**

The VAT from the sales daybook is payable to HMRC, whereas the VAT from the sales returns and the purchases daybooks can be reclaimed. It is the net effect that is payable to HMRC.

Businesses are required to complete a VAT return, usually on a quarterly basis, to show the amount payable to or reclaimed from the tax authorities (HMRC). Whilst you are not required to complete the return itself, you may be told of the amount showing on the VAT return and asked to confirm if it agrees to the control account calculated.

Test your understanding 6

The following VAT figures have been extracted from the books of prime entry.

Sales day book	60,200
Sales returns day book	980
Purchases day book	34,300
Purchases returns day book	2,660
Cash receipts book	112
Discounts allowed day book	640
Discounts received day book	450

(a) Show the entries in the VAT control account to record the VAT transactions in the quarter.

(b) The VAT return has been completed and shows an amount owing from the tax authorities of £27,502. Is the VAT return correct?

 Test your understanding 7

This quarter Sasha had net sales of £189,500, made purchases inclusive of VAT of £240,000 and had some returns made by customers amounting to £1,880 excluding VAT.

Draw up the VAT control account for Sasha, stating clearly whether the closing balance is payable to HMRC or receivable from them.

KAPLAN PUBLISHING

Test your understanding 8

The following totals are taken from the books of a business:

	£
Credit balance on purchases ledger control account	5,926
Debit balance on sales ledger control account	10,268
Credit sales	71,504
Credit purchases	47,713
Cash received from credit customers	69,872
Cash paid to payables	47,028
Sales ledger balances written off as bad	96
Sales returns	358
Purchases returns	202
Discounts allowed	1,435
Discounts received	867
Contra entry	75

Required:

(a) Prepare the purchases ledger control account and balance at the end of the month.

(b) Prepare the sales ledger control account and balance at the end of the month.

 Test your understanding 9

The balance on the sales ledger control account of Robin & Co on 30 September 20X0 amounted to £3,825 which did not agree with the net total of the list of sales ledger balances at that date of £3,362.

The errors discovered were as follows:

1 Debit balances in the sales ledger, amounting to £103, had been omitted from the list of balances.

2 An irrecoverable debt amounting to £400 had been written off in the sales ledger but had not been posted to the irrecoverable debts expense account or entered in the control accounts.

3 An item of goods sold to Sparrow, £250, had been entered once in the sales day book but posted to his account twice.

4   No entry had been made in the control account in respect of the transfer of a debit of £70 from Quail's account in the sales ledger to his account in the purchases ledger (a contra entry).

5   The discount allowed column in the discount allowed daybook had been undercast by £140.

Required:

(a)   Make the necessary adjustments in the sales ledger control account and bring down the balance.

(b)   Show the adjustments to the net total of the original list of balances to reconcile with the amended balance on the sales ledger control account.

 Test your understanding 10

When carrying out the purchases ledger control account reconciliation the following errors were discovered:

(a)   the purchases day book was overcast by £1,000

(b)   the total of the discount received column in the discounts received daybook was posted to the general ledger as £89 instead of £98

(c)   a contra entry of £300 had been entered in the subsidiary ledger but not in the general ledger.

Required:

Produce journal entries to correct each of these errors.

---

7   Summary

This chapter has looked at control account reconciliations. The entries into the SLCA and PLCA are items that students should be comfortable with, but the process of reconciling this to the subsidiary ledgers can be a tricky one. This process uses knowledge of errors taken from chapter 4, so it is important to be comfortable with the types of errors that could arise.

Students must be able to process the entries in addition to verifying whether the balance represents a liability to HMRC or an asset due from them.

Test your understanding answers

 Test your understanding 1

(a) Yes, because the correct entries in the sales day book are posted to the sales ledger and the incorrect total used in control account.

(b) No, because the arithmetical balance is correct.

(c) No, because the total posted to the SLCA will include the £67 and the entry in the sales ledger will also be for £67.

 Test your understanding 2

- We must first look for those errors which will mean that the SLCA is incorrectly stated. The control account is then adjusted as follows:

Sales ledger control account

	£		£
Balance b/d	15,450	Discounts allowed	70
		Overcast of sales day book	200
		Contra with PLCA	40
		Adjusted balance c/d	15,140
	———		———
	15,450		15,450
	———		———
Balance b/d	15,140		

- We then look for errors in the total of individual balances per the sales ledger. The list of balances must be adjusted as follows:

Original total of list of balances	15,705
Debit balance omitted	65
Transposition error (810 – 180)	(630)
	———
	15,140
	———

- As can be seen, the adjusted total of the list of balances now agrees with the balance per the control account.

Test your understanding 3

- We must first look for those errors which will mean that the sales ledger control account is incorrectly stated. The control account is then adjusted as follows:

Sales ledger control account

	£		£
Balance b/d	18,971.12	Discounts allowed	10.00
Undercast of sales day book	1,500.00		
		Adjusted balance c/d	20,461.12
	20,471.12		20,471.12
Balance b/d	20,461.12		

- We must then look for errors in the total of the individual balances per the sales ledger. The extracted list of balances must be adjusted as follows:

	£
Original total of list of balances	21,761.12
Invoice duplication	(300.00)
Omission of credit note	(1,000.00)
	20,461.12

- As can be seen, the adjusted total of the list of balances now agrees with the balance per the control account.

 Test your understanding 4

(a) This does not affect the reconciliation. A correction would simply be made in the subsidiary ledger.

(b) This must be adjusted for in the purchase ledger control account and in the purchases ledger.

(c) This is just an adjustment to the purchase ledger control account.

(d) This will require alteration in both the control account and the purchases ledger.

KAPLAN PUBLISHING

Test your understanding 5

TRANSACTION	Amount (£)	DEBIT ✓	CREDIT ✓
Balance brought down	60,980	✓	
Goods sold on credit	12,566	✓	
Returns made by credit customers	4,224		✓
Payments made by credit customers	15,789		✓
Discounts allowed	569		✓
Irrecoverable debt written off	872		✓

The balance carried down will be **£52,092**

Balance per control account:	**£52,092**
Balance per subsidiary ledgers:	**£52,964**
Difference:	**£872**

The difference may have been caused by irrecoverable debts being omitted from the subsidiary ledger. As these have been omitted, the subsidiary ledger is £872 higher than the control account.

Test your understanding 6

(a)   **VAT account**

Details	Amount £	Details	Amount £
Sales Returns (SRDB)	980	Sales (SDB)	60,200
Purchases (PDB)	34,300	Purchases returns	2,660
Discounts allowed day book	640	Cash sales (CRB)	112
		Discounts received	450
Balance c/d	27,502		
	63,422		**63,422**
		Balance b/d	27,502

(b)   No. The amount of £27,502 is payable to the tax authorities.

Test your understanding 7

(a)   **VAT account**

Details	Amount £	Details	Amount £
Purchases	40,000	Sales	37,900
Sales returns	376		
		Balance c/d	2,476
	40,376		**40,376**
Balance b/d	2,476		

(b)   The amount of £2,476 is reclaimable from the tax authorities.

Test your understanding 8

(a)

Purchases ledger control account

	£		£
Cash paid	47,028	Balance b/d	5,926
Purchases returns	202	Purchases (total from PDB)	47,713
Discounts received	867		
Sales ledger control account (contra)	75		
Balance c/d (bal fig)	5,467		
	53,639		53,639

(b)

Sales ledger control account

	£		£
Balance b/d	10,268	Bank account	69,872
Sales (total from SDB)	71,504	Irrecoverable debts account	96
		Sales returns account (total from SRDB)	358
		Discounts allowed	1,435
		Purchases ledger control account (contra)	75
		Balance c/d (bal fig)	9,936
	81,772		81,772

Test your understanding 9

(a) **Sales ledger control account**

	£		£
30 Sep Balance b/d	3,825	Irrecoverable debts (2)	400
		PLCA (4)	70
		Discount allowed (5)	140
		Balance c/d	3,215
	3,825		3,825
1 Oct Balance b/d	3,215		

(b) **List of sales ledger balances**

	£
Original total	3,362
Add: Debit balances previously omitted (1)	103
	3,465
Less: Item posted twice to Sparrow's account (3)	(250)
Amended total agreeing with SLCA	3,215

Test your understanding 10

(a)

Account name	Amount £	Dr ✓	Cr ✓
Purchase ledger control account	1,000.00	✓	
Purchases	1,000.00		✓

(b)

Account name	Amount £	Dr ✓	Cr ✓
Purchase ledger control account	9.00	✓	
Discounts received	9.00		✓

(c)

Account name	Amount £	Dr ✓	Cr ✓
Purchase ledger control account	300.00	✓	
Sales ledger control account	300.00		✓

Payroll procedures

Introduction

We have previously seen how payments by cheque and other methods are made from the bank account for purchases and expenses. In this chapter we will consider one of the most significant payments that most businesses will make either weekly or monthly – wages and salaries.

ASSESSMENT CRITERIA
Produce journal entries to record accounting transactions (4.1)

CONTENTS

1 Overview of the payroll function

1.1 Introduction

The payroll system in a business is one of the most important. The payroll staff not only have a responsibility to calculate correctly the amount of pay due to each employee but they must also ensure that each employee is paid on time with the correct amount and that amounts due to external parties such as HM Revenue and Customs are correctly determined and paid on time.

There are many facets to the payroll function and each will be briefly covered as an introduction in this section and then considered in more detail in later sections of the chapter.

1.2 Calculation of gross pay

The initial calculation that must be carried out for each employee is the calculation of the employee's gross pay. Gross pay is the wage or salary due to the employee for the amount of work done in the period which may be a week or a month depending upon how frequently the employees are paid.

Gross pay may depend upon a number of factors:

- basic hours worked
- overtime hours worked
- bonus
- commission
- holiday pay
- sick pay.

1.3 Deductions

Once the gross pay for each employee has been determined then a number of deductions from this amount will be made to arrive at the net pay for the employee. Net pay is the amount that the employee will actually receive.

Some deductions are compulsory or statutory:

- Income tax in the form of PAYE.
- National Insurance Contributions (NIC) which can also be referred to as social security payments.

Other deductions are at the choice of the employer or employee and are therefore non-statutory:

- Save as you earn

- Give as you earn

- Pension contributions.

1.4 Payment of wages or salaries

Once the net pay has been determined then each employee must be paid the correct amount, by the most appropriate method at the correct time.

1.5 Payments to external agencies

As you will see later in the chapter employers deduct income tax and NIC from each employee's wages or salaries and the employer must also pay its own NIC contribution for each employee. This is done by making payment to HM Revenue and Customs on a regular basis and this is therefore another responsibility of the payroll function.

1.6 Accounting for wages and salaries

Finally once the wages and salaries for the period have been paid then the amounts involved must be correctly entered into the ledger accounts.

1.7 Accuracy and confidentiality

Whilst carrying out all of these calculations and functions it is obviously important that the calculations are made with total accuracy. Not only is the amount that each individual will be paid dependent upon these calculations but there is a statutory duty to make the correct deductions from gross pay and to pay these over to HM Revenue and Customs.

Payroll staff deal with confidential and sensitive information about individuals such as the rate of pay for an individual. It is of the utmost importance that such details are kept confidential and are not made public nor allowed to be accessed by unauthorised personnel.

2 Gross pay

2.1 Introduction

Gross pay is the total amount payable to the employee before any deductions have been made. Gross pay can be made up of many different elements, e.g.

- normal wages or salary

- overtime

- shift payments

- bonus

- commission

- holiday pay

- statutory sick pay (or SSP) and

- statutory maternity pay (or SMP).

2.2 Wages and salaries

These are fairly straightforward. Employees will have an agreed monthly, weekly or hourly rate.

The monthly and weekly rates will not need any further calculations.

However, for hourly paid employees calculations will be needed for the total earnings. The source of this information might be clock cards.

 Definition

A clock card is a card which records the hours worked by an employee.

As the employee arrives or leaves they put their card in the slot of a special clock. The mechanism inside the clock stamps the time on the card.

The payroll clerk would transfer the number of hours worked onto special calculation sheets.

2.3 Overtime and shift payments

These need to be identified so that the payroll clerk can calculate the amount payable.

Overtime is hours worked which are over and above the agreed number of weekly or monthly hours for that employee. For example, it may be agreed that an employee has a standard working week of 38 hours. If he works for 42 hours in a week then he has worked 4 hours of overtime.

Overtime or shifts worked might be recorded on:

- clock cards
- timesheets or
- authorisation forms (signed by the employee's supervisor).

Some employees are paid at a higher rate for overtime. They might be paid at one and a half times the normal rate. This is called time and a half.

Twice the normal rate is double time.

Some employees might be paid premium rates or bonuses for working certain shifts.

2.4 Bonus and commission payments

The business may pay certain employees a bonus. This bonus may be for achieving a particular target.

Company directors often receive a bonus if the company achieves certain profits.

Companies with a large number of sales representatives may pay their sales representatives a commission as part of their salary. This commission is based on the value of the sales they make.

For instance, a salesman might be paid a basic salary of £10,000 a year plus a 1% commission on sales that he makes.

2.5 Holiday pay

Most employers pay their employees even while they are on holiday.

If the employee is paid monthly, then there is no problem. The employee is paid the usual amount at the normal time.

If the employee is paid weekly, they would prefer to be paid for the holiday period in advance. This means that if the employee is taking two weeks' holiday they will have to be paid three weeks' wages at once.

2.6 Statutory sick pay (SSP) and statutory maternity pay (SMP)

For Bookkeeping Controls you will really only need to be concerned about basic wages and salaries, overtime and bonus payments.

If there is a reference to SSP or SMP you will be told how to deal with it.

3 Income tax

3.1 Introduction

Everybody in the UK has a potential liability to pay tax on their income.

Individuals pay **income tax**. The rate of tax depends on the amount of their income.

Definition

Income tax is a tax on individuals' income.

3.2 Tax-free income

Everybody is entitled to some tax-free income.

This tax-free sum is known as the personal allowance.

Definition

The personal allowance is an amount which an individual is allowed to earn tax-free.

3.3 How income tax is paid

Employees in the UK pay their income tax through the **PAYE** (or Pay As You Earn) **scheme**.

Definition

The PAYE scheme is a national scheme whereby employers withhold tax and other deductions from their employees' wages and salaries when they are paid. The deductions are then paid over monthly to HM Revenue and Customs by the employer.

Looking at tax alone, the main advantages of this scheme are:

- employees pay the tax as they earn the income

- most people do not have to complete a tax return unless they have several different sources of income

- employers act as unpaid tax collectors (this is a serious responsibility and they can be fined for mistakes) and

- the government receives a steady stream of revenue throughout the year.

 Test your understanding 1

Under the PAYE Scheme who pays over the income tax to the Collector of Taxes?

A   The employee

B   The employer

C   The government

D   The Inspector of Taxes

 National Insurance/Pension contributions

4.1   What is National Insurance?

National Insurance is a state scheme which pays certain benefits including:

- retirement pensions

- widow's allowances and pensions

- jobseeker's allowance

- incapacity benefit and

- maternity allowance.

The scheme is run by HM Revenue and Customs.

The scheme is funded by people who are currently in employment.

Most people in employment (including partners in partnerships, and sole traders) who have earnings above a certain level must pay National Insurance contributions.

4.2 Types of National Insurance contributions

Both the employer and the employee pay National Insurance contributions.

(a) **Employees' National Insurance contributions**

The employer deducts National Insurance contributions from an employee's weekly wage or monthly salary, and pays these to HM Revenue and Customs. Income tax and National Insurance contributions are both taxes on income, but they have different historical origins and are calculated in different ways. Employees' National Insurance is now, however, similar to income tax in many respects, and is really a form of income tax with another name.

Like income tax, employees' NI contributions are deducted from pay. The amount of the contributions an employee pays is linked to his or her earnings, and is obtained by reference to National Insurance tables supplied by HM Revenue and Customs.

You are not required to know how to use NI tables.

(b) **Employer's National Insurance contributions**

In addition to deducting employees' National Insurance contributions from each employee's wages or salary, an employer is required to pay the employer's National Insurance contributions for each employee. The amount payable for each employee is linked to the size of his or her earnings.

Employer's National Insurance contributions are therefore an employment tax. They are not deducted from the employee's gross pay. They are an additional cost of payroll to the employer, paid for by the employer rather than the employee.

4.3 Pension contributions

Both the employer and the employee may make contributions to a pension scheme.

(a) **Employees' pension contributions**

The employer deducts pension contributions from an employee's weekly wage or monthly salary, and pays these to the pension provider.

(b) **Employer's pension contributions**

Similar to the employer's national insurance contributions, the employer's pension contributions are an additional cost of payroll to the employer, paid for by the employer rather than the employee.

5 Other deductions

5.1 Deductions

The employee may also choose to have further deductions made from their gross pay. These include:

- payments under the **save as you earn scheme**; this is a strictly governed scheme offered by some employers that allows you to save a regular amount each pay day. You would use this money to buy shares in the company at a later date.

- payments under the **give as you earn scheme**; this scheme allows employees to request that their employer withhold a certain amount from their salary and pay it over to a charity, on their behalf.

- other payments, e.g. subscriptions to sports and social clubs and trade unions.

5.2 Summary of deductions and payments

It is time to summarise what deductions the employer makes from the employee's gross salary, and to whom the employer makes the various payments.

To process the payroll an employer must, **for each employee**:

- calculate the gross wage or salary for the period

- calculate the income tax payable out of these earnings

- calculate the employee's National Insurance contributions that are deductible

- calculate any non-statutory deductions

- calculate the employer's National Insurance contributions.

The employer must then:

- make the payment of net pay to each employee

- make the payments of all the non-statutory deductions from pay to the appropriate other organisations

- pay the employee's PAYE, the employee's NIC and the employer's NIC to HM Revenue and Customs for all employees.

Example 1

John earns £12,000 per annum. His PAYE, NIC and other deductions and the employer's NIC for the month of May 20X4 are:

	£
PAYE	125
Employee's NIC	80
Employee contribution to personal pension scheme	50
Employer's NIC	85

Calculate:

(a) John's net pay

(b) the cost to the employer of employing John

(c) the amounts to be paid to the various organisations involved.

Solution

			Paid by employer to:
Gross pay per month		1,000	
Less: PAYE	125		HMRC
Employee's NIC	80		HMRC
Personal pension	50		Pension company
		(255)	
Net pay		745	John
Employer's NIC	85		HMRC

(a) John's net pay is £745.

(b) The cost of employing John is (1,000 + 85) = £1,085.

(c) The pension company is paid £50 by the employer.

HM Revenue and Customs is paid £290 by the employer:

	£
PAYE	125
Employee's NIC	80
Employer's NIC	85
	290

Where there are many employees, the employer will pay the amounts calculated per (c) above for all employees to HM Revenue and Customs with one cheque.

6 Payroll accounting procedures

6.1 Introduction

The accounting for wages and salaries is based upon two fundamental principles:

- the accounts must reflect the full cost to the employer of employing someone (which is their gross pay plus the employer's NI contribution)

- the accounts must show the payable for PAYE and NIC that must be paid over to HM Revenue and Customs on a regular basis, usually monthly.

We therefore need two accounts, plus a third control account.

(a) The wages expense account which shows the full cost of employing the staff.

(b) The HMRC Liability account which shows the amount to be paid to HM Revenue and Customs.

(c) The wages and salaries control account which acts as a control over the entries in the accounts. There are different ways of writing up this control account, but the way used by AAT is to use this account to control the gross pay and deductions from the employees, plus employers' NIC.

6.2 Double entry

The double entry reflects these two fundamentals and uses three main accounts – the wages and salaries control account, the wages expense account and the HMRC liability account.

1 Dr Wages expense account

      Cr Wages and salaries control account

with the total expenses relating to the business (gross pay plus employer's NIC)

2 Dr Wages and salaries control account

      Cr Bank account

with the net wages paid to the employees

3 Dr Wages and salaries control account

      Cr HMRC Liability

with those deductions made from the employees which are payable to the HM Revenue and Customs

Example 2

The wages and salaries information for an organisation for a week is given as follows:

	£
Gross wages	34,000
PAYE deducted	7,400
NIC deducted	5,600
Net pay	21,000
Employer's NIC	7,800

Write up the relevant ledger accounts in the general ledger to reflect this.

Solution

Wages and salaries control account

		£			£
2	Bank account	21,000	1	Wages expense account	34,000
3	HMRC Liability (PAYE)	7,400		(Gross pay)	
3	HMRC Liability (ees NIC)	5,600	1	Wages expense account	7,800
3	HMRC Liability (ers NIC)	7,800		(ers NIC)	
		41,800			41,800

Wages expense account

	£		£
1 Wages and salaries control (Gross pay)	34,000		
1 Wages and salaries control (ers NIC)	7,800		
		Bal c/d	41,800
	41,800		41,800

HMRC Liability

	£				£
		3	Wages and salaries control		7,400
		3	Wages and salaries control		5,600
Bal c/d	20,800	3	Wages and salaries control		7,800
	20,800				20,800
			Bal b/d		20,800

6.3 Commentary on the solution

(a) The wages and salaries control account controls the total gross wages plus the employer's NIC and the amounts paid to the employees, and other organisations (e.g.HM Revenue and Customs for PAYE and NIC). The total gross pay is taken from the company payroll as are the deductions. Assuming that the company payroll schedule reconciles and no errors are made when posting the payroll totals to the account, the account should have a nil balance.

(b) The wages expense account shows the total cost to the employer of employing the workforce (£41,800). This is the gross wages cost plus the employer's own NIC cost.

(c) The HMRC Liability account shows the amount due to be paid over to HMRC, i.e. PAYE, employee's NIC plus the employer's NIC.

 Test your understanding 2

Given below is a summary of an organisation's payroll details for a week.

	£
Gross wages	54,440
PAYE	11,840
Employee's NIC	8,960
Employer's NIC	12,480

You are required to prepare the journals to enter the figures in the general ledger accounts and to state the balance on the control account, once the net amount has been paid to the employees.

 Test your understanding 3

Steph earns £36,000 per annum. Her deductions for the month are:

	£
PAYE	530
Employee's NIC	275
Employer's pension contributions	100
Employee contribution to pension	100
Employer's NIC	350

Based on the information given, write up the wages expense, wages control, HMRC liability and pension liability accounts.

Test your understanding 4

Miss Maynard pays her employees by cheque every month and maintains a wages control account. A summary of last month's payroll transactions is shown below:

Item	£
Gross wages	35,000
Employers' NIC	4,200
Employees' NIC	2,970
Income tax	8,213
Employer pension	2,000
Employee pension	1,010

Record the journal entries needed in the general ledger to:

(i) Record the wages expense

(ii) Record the HM Revenue and Customs liability

(iii) Record the net wages paid to the employees

(iv) Record the pension liability.

 Test your understanding 5

An employee has gross pay for a week of £368.70. The PAYE for the week is £46.45, the employer's NIC £30.97 and the employee's NIC £23.96.

What is the employee's net pay for the week?

Test your understanding 6

Given below is the wages book for the month of May 20X1 for a small business with four employees.

Wages book

Employee number	Gross pay	PAYE	Employee's NIC	Employer's NIC	Net pay
	£	£	£	£	£
001	1,200	151	78	101	971
002	1,400	176	91	118	1,133
003	900	113	58	76	729
004	1,550	195	101	130	1,254
	5,050	635	328	425	4,087

You are required to use the totals from the wages book for the month to write up journal entries to record:

- the wages expense

- the HM Revenue and Customs liability

- the net wages paid to the employees.

You can then record these entries in the ledger accounts below.

Gross wages control account

	£			£

Wages expense account

		£			£
30 April	Balance b/d	23,446			

HM Revenue and Customs account

		£			£
19 May	CPB	760	30 April	Balance b/d	760

7 Summary

This chapter has introduced the fairly complex taxation elements that affect the payment of wages and salaries. You need to understand in principle how PAYE and NI works and be able to calculate the net pay to employees given the PAYE and NI deductions. However, you do not need to be able to use HM Revenue and Customs tables. Most importantly you do need to understand how wages and salaries are accounted for in the general ledger.

Test your understanding answers

Test your understanding 1

B   The employer

Test your understanding 2

1   Dr   Wages expense account

      Cr   Wages and salaries control account

With the total expense of £66,920

2   Dr   Wages and salaries control account

      Cr   HMRC Liability account

with the PAYE of £11,840, and with the employee's NIC of £8,960 and with the employer's NIC of £12,480.

Once the net amount to be paid to the employee has been posted by debiting the wages and salaries control account and crediting the bank account with £33,640, the balance on the control account will be nil.

Test your understanding 3

Solution

Wages and salaries control account

	£		£
Bank account	2,095	Wages expense account	3,450
HMRC Liability (PAYE + both NIC)	1,155		
Pension liability	200		
	3,450		3,450

Wages expense account

	£		£
Wages and salaries control (Gross + Er's NIC + Er's pension)	3,450		
		Bal c/d	3,450
	3,450		3,450

HMRC liability

	£		£
		Wages and salaries control	1,155
Bal c/d	1,155		
	1,155		1,155

Pension liability

	£		£
		Wages and salaries control	200
Bal c/d	200		
	200		200

Test your understanding 4

(i)

Account name	Amount £	Debit ✓	Credit ✓
Wages expense	41,200	✓	
Wages control	41,200		✓

(ii)

Account name	Amount £	Debit ✓	Credit ✓
Wages control	15,383	✓	
HMRC liability	15,383		✓

(iii)

Account name	Amount £	Debit ✓	Credit ✓
Wages control	22,807	✓	
Bank	22,807		✓

(iv)

Account name	Amount £	Debit ✓	Credit ✓
Wages control	3,010	✓	
Pension	3,010		✓

Test your understanding 5

	£
Gross pay	368.70
Less: PAYE	(46.45)
NIC	(23.96)
Net pay	298.29

Test your understanding 6

Account name	Amount £	Dr ✓	Cr ✓
Wages expense	5,475	✓	
Wages control	5,475		✓

Account name	Amount £	Dr ✓	Cr ✓
HM Revenue and Customs	1,388		✓
Wages control	1,388	✓	

Account name	Amount £	Dr ✓	Cr ✓
Bank	4,087		✓
Wages control	4,087	✓	

Gross wages control account

		£			£
31 May	Net pay – Bank	4,087	31 May	Gross – wages expense	5,050
	PAYE – HMRC	635	31 May	Emp'ers NIC – wages exp	425
	Emp'ees NIC – HMRC	328			
	Empl'ers NIC – HMRC	425			
		5,475			5,475

Wages expense account

		£			£
30 Apr	Balance b/d	23,446			
31 May	Gross – wages control	5,050			
	Emp'ers NIC – control	425	31 May	Balance c/d	28,921
		28,921			28,921
31 May	Balance b/d	28,921			

HM Revenue and Customs account

		£			£
19 May	CPB	760	30 Apr	Balance b/d	760
			31 May	PAYE – wages control	635
				Emp'ees NIC – control	328
31 May	Balance c/d	1,388		Emp'ers NIC – control	425
		2,148			2,148
			31 May	Balance b/d	1,388

Bank reconciliations

7

Introduction

Completion of this chapter will ensure we are able to correctly prepare the cash book, compare the entries in the cash book to details on the bank statement and then finally to prepare a bank reconciliation statement.

ASSESSMENT CRITERIA

Locate differences between items on the bank statement and entries in the cash book (5.1)

Use the bank statement to update the cash book (5.2)

Produce a bank reconciliation statement (5.3)

CONTENTS

1 Writing up the cash book
2 Preparing the bank reconciliation statement
3 Returned cheques

1 Writing up the cash book

1.1 Introduction

We were introduced to the cash book within Bookkeeping Transactions and will review it now for Bookkeeping Controls.

Most businesses will have a separate cash receipts book and a cash payments book which form part of the double entry system. If this form of record is used, the cash balance must be calculated from the opening balance at the beginning of the period, plus the receipts shown in the cash receipts book for the period and minus the payments shown in the cash payments book for the period.

1.2 Balancing the cash book

The following brief calculation will enable us to find the balance on the cash book when separate receipts and payments book are maintained.

	£
Opening balance per the cash book	X
Add: Receipts in the period	X
Less: Payments in the period	(X)
Closing balance per the cash book	X

☀ Example 1

Suppose that the opening balance on the cash book is £358.72 on 1 June. During June the cash payments book shows that there were total payments made of £7,326.04 during the month of June and the cash receipts book shows receipts for the month of £8,132.76.

What is the closing balance on the cash book at the end of June?

Solution

		£
Opening balance at 1 June		358.72
Add:	Receipts for June	8,132.76
Less:	Payments for June	(7,326.04)
Balance at 30 June		1,165.44

Take care if the opening balance on the cash book is an overdraft balance. Any receipts in the period will reduce the overdraft and any payments will increase the overdraft.

Suppose that the opening balance on the cash book is £631.25 overdrawn on 1 June. During June the cash payments book shows that there were total payments made of £2,345.42 during the month of June and the cash receipts book shows receipts for the month of £1,276.45.

What is the closing balance on the cash book at the end of June?

Solution

		£
Opening balance at 1 June		(631.25)
Add:	Receipts for June	1,276.45
Less:	Payments for June	(2,345.42)
		———
Balance at 30 June		(1,700.22)
		———

 Test your understanding 1

The opening balance at 1 January in a business cash book was £673.42 overdrawn. During January payments totalled £6,419.37 and receipts totalled £6,488.20.

What is the closing balance on the cash book?

---

2 Preparing the bank reconciliation statement

2.1   Introduction

At regular intervals (normally at least once a month) the cashier must check that the cash book is correct by comparing the cash book with the bank statement.

2.2 Differences between the cash book and bank statement

At any date the balance shown on the bank statement is unlikely to agree with the balance in the cash book for two main reasons.

(a) **Items in the cash book not on the bank statement**

Certain items will have been entered in the cash book but will not appear on the bank statement at the time of the reconciliation. Examples are:

- cheques received by the business and paid into the bank which have not yet appeared on the bank statement, due to the time lag of the clearing system. These are known as **outstanding lodgements** (can also be referred to as "uncleared lodgements").

- cheques written by the business but which have not yet appeared on the bank statement, because the recipients have not yet paid them in, or the cheques are in the clearing system. These are known as **unpresented cheques**.

- errors in the cash book (e.g. transposition of numbers, addition errors).

(b) **Items on the bank statement not in the cash book**

At the time of the bank reconciliation certain items will appear on the bank statement that have not yet been entered into the cash book. These can occur due to the cashier not being aware of the existence of these items until receiving the bank statements. Examples are:

- direct debit or standing order payments that are in the bank statement but have not yet been entered in the cash payments book.

- BACS or other receipts paid directly into the bank account by a customer.

- bank charges or bank interest that are unknown until the bank statement has been received and therefore will not be in the cash book.

- errors in the cash book that may only come to light when the cash book entries are compared to the bank statement.

- returned cheques i.e. cheques paid in from a customer who does not have sufficient funds in his bank to pay the cheque (see later in this chapter).

2.3 The bank reconciliation

 Definition

Definition: A bank reconciliation is simply a statement that explains the differences between the balance in the cash book and the balance on the bank statement at a particular date.

A bank reconciliation is produced by following a standard set of steps.

Step 1: Compare the cash book and the bank statement for the relevant period and identify any differences between them.

You should begin with agreeing the opening balances on the bank statement and cash book so that you are aware of any prior period reconciling items that exist.

This is usually done by ticking in the cash book and bank statement items that appear in both the cash book and the bank statement. Any items left unticked therefore only appear in one place, either the cash book or the bank statement. We saw in 2.2 above the reasons why this might occur.

Step 2: Update the cash book for any items that appear on the bank statement that have not yet been entered into the cash book.

Tick these items in both the cash book and the bank statement once they are entered in the cash book.

At this stage there will be no unticked items on the bank statement.

(You clearly cannot enter on the bank statement items in the cash book that do not appear on the bank statement – the bank prepares the bank statement, not you. These items will either be unpresented cheques or outstanding lodgements – see 2.2 above.)

Step 3: Bring down the new cash book balance following the adjustments in step 2 above.

Step 4: Prepare the bank reconciliation statement.

This will typically have the following proforma.

Bank reconciliation as at 31.0X.200X

	£
Balance as per bank statement	X
Less unpresented cheques	(X)
Add outstanding lodgements	X
Balance as per cash book	X

Think for a moment to ensure you understand this proforma.

We deduct the unpresented cheques (cheques already entered in the cash book but not yet on the bank statement) from the bank balance, because when they are presented this bank balance will be reduced.

We add outstanding lodgements (cash received and already entered in the cash book) because when they appear on the bank statement they will increase the bank balance.

It is also useful to remember that the bank reconciliation can be performed the opposite way round as shown below:

Bank reconciliation as at 31.0X.200X

	£
Balance as per cash book	X
Add unpresented cheques	(X)
Less outstanding lodgements	X
Balance as per bank statement	X

If we start with the cash book balance, to reconcile this to the bank statement balance we add back the unpresented cheques as though they haven't been paid out of the cash book (as the bank statement has not recognised these being paid out).

We deduct outstanding lodgements as though we haven't recognised these in the cash book (as the bank statement has not recognised these receipts). The cash book balance should then agree to the bank statement balance i.e. we have reconciled these balances.

2.4   Debits and credits in bank statements

When comparing the cash book to the bank statement it is easy to get confused with debits and credits.

- When we pay money into the bank, we debit our cash book but the bank credits our account.

- This is because a debit in our cash book represents the increase in our asset 'cash'. For the bank, the situation is different: they will debit their cash book and credit our account because they now owe us more money; we are a payable.

- When our account is overdrawn, we owe the bank money and consequently our cash book will show a credit balance. For the bank an overdraft is a debit balance.

On the bank statement a credit is an amount of money paid into the account and a debit represents a payment. A bank statement conveys the transactions in the bank's point of view rather than the business' point of view.

 Example 2

On 30 April Tomasso's received the following bank statement as at 28 April.

Today's date is 30 April.

	QC Bank			
	QC Street, London			
To: Tomasso's	Account No 92836152			30 April 2012

Date	Details	Debit	Credit	Balance
2012		£	£	£
2 April	Bal b/f			100 C
3 April	Cheque 101	55		45 C
4 April	Cheque 103	76		31 D
6 April	Bank Giro Credit		1,000	969 C
9 April	Cheque 105	43		926 C
10 April	Cheque 106	12		914 C
11 April	Cheque 107	98		816 C
21 April	Direct Debit RBC	100		716 C
22 April	Direct Debit OPO	150		566 C
23 April	Interest received		30	596 C
24 April	Bank charges	10		586 C
28 April	Bank Giro Credit DJA		250	836 C

The cash book at 28 April is shown below.

Date 2012	Details	Bank £	Date 2012	Cheque number	Details	Bank £
	Balance b/f	100	01 April	101	Alan & Co	55
06 April	Prance Dance Co.	1,000	02 April	102	Amber's	99
23 April	Interest received	30	02 April	103	Kiki & Company	76
23 April	Graham Interiors	2,000	05 April	104	Marta	140
25 April	Italia Design	900	06 April	105	Nina Ltd	43
			07 April	106	Willy Wink	12
			08 April	107	Xylophones	98

Firstly, we see that the opening balance is £100 per both the bank statement and the cash book. Secondly, we must tick off the items in the bank statement to the cash book.

The effect of this on the bank statement can be seen below.

Date	Details	Debit £	Credit £	Balance £
2 April	Bal b/f			100 C
3 April	Cheque 101	✓55		45 C
4 April	Cheque 103	✓76		31 D
6 April	Bank Giro Credit		✓1,000	969 C
9 April	Cheque 105	✓43		926 C
10 April	Cheque 106	✓12		914 C
11 April	Cheque 107	✓98		816 C
21 April	Direct Debit RBC	100		716 C
22 April	Direct Debit OPO	150		566 C
23 April	Interest received		✓30	596 C
24 April	Bank charges	10		586 C
28 April	Bank Giro Credit DJA		250	836 C

This leaves 4 unticked items. The cash book is then updated for these below.

Date 2012	Details	Bank £	Date 2012	Cheque number	Details	Bank £
	Balance b/d	100	01 April	101	Alan & Co	✓55
06 April	Prance Dance Co.	✓1,000	02 April	102	Amber's	99
23 April	Interest received	✓30	02 April	103	Kiki & Company	✓76
23 April	Graham Interiors	2,000	05 April	104	Marta	140
25 April	Italia Design	900	06 April	105	Nina Ltd	✓43
28 April	DJA	250	07 April	106	Willy Wink	✓12
			08 April	107	Xylophones	✓98
			21 April	–	DD – RBC	100
			22 April	–	DD – OPO	150
			24 April	–	Bank charges	10
			28 April	–	Balance c/d	3,497
		4,280				4,280
29 April	Balance b/d	3,497				

Once the cash book has been updated, there are 4 remaining unticked items.

These are the items that will go onto the bank reconciliation, as shown below.

Bank reconciliation statement as at 28 April	£
Balance per bank statement	836
Add:	
Name: Graham's Interior	2,000
Name: Italia Design	900
Total to add	2,900
Less:	
Name: Amber's	99
Name: Marta	140
Total to subtract	239
Balance as per cash book	3,497

Test your understanding 2

Below is a bank statement for Alpha Ltd at 31 May 2012.

Bark Lays Bank plc
High Street, London SE8 1ND

To: Alpha Ltd   Account No 48774900   31 May 2012

Date	Details	Debit	Credit	Balance
2012		£	£	£
1 May	Bal b/d			886 D
3 May	Cheque no 0041	2,000		2,886 D
6 May	Bank Giro Credit		360	2,526 D
7 May	Cheque no 0043	840		3,366 D
10 May	BACS		6,200	2,834 C
10 May	Credit		630	3,464 C
10 May	Credit		880	4,344 C
25 May	Bank Interest		40	4,384 C
31 May	BACS		460	4,844 C
		D = Debit	C= Credit	

Alpha's cash book for the month of May is shown below.

Date 2012	Details	Bank £	Date 2012	Cheque number	Details	Bank £
			1 May		Balance b/d	526
6 May	Shaws	630	3 May	0041	Bills Farm	2,000
6 May	Andrew Ltd	880	3 May	0042	Cows Head	3,240
			5 May	0043	Adam Ant	840
			30 May	0044	Miles to Go	700

Update Alpha's cash book.

2.5   Opening balances disagree

Usually the balances on the bank statement and in the cash book do not agree at the start of the period for the same reasons that they do not agree at the end, e.g. items in the cash book that were not on the bank statement. When producing the reconciliation statement it is important to take this opening difference into account.

Example 3

The bank statement and cash book of Jones for the month of December 20X8 start as follows.

Bank statement

		Debit £	Credit £	Balance £
1 Dec 20X8	Balance b/d (favourable)			8,570
2 Dec 20X8	0073	125		
2 Dec 20X8	0074	130		
3 Dec 20X8	Sundries		105	

Cash book

	£			£
1 Dec 20X8 b/d	8,420	Cheque 0075	Wages	200
Sales	320	Cheque 0076	Rent	500
	X			X
	X			X

Required:

Explain the difference between the opening balances.

Solution

The difference in the opening balance is as follows.

£8,570 – £8,420 = £150

This difference is due to the following.

	£
Cheque 0073	125
Cheque 0074	130
	———
	255
Lodgement (sundries)	(105)
	———
	150
	———

These cheques and lodgements were in the cash book in November, but only appear on the bank statement in December. They will therefore be matched and ticked against the entries in the November cash book. The December reconciliation will then proceed as normal.

3 Returned cheques

A customer C may send a cheque in payment of an invoice without having sufficient funds in his account with Bank A.

The seller S who receives the cheque will pay it into his account with Bank B and it will go into the clearing system. Bank B will credit S's account with the funds in anticipation of the cheque being honoured.

Bank A however will not pay funds into the S's account with Bank B and Bank B will then remove the funds from S's account.

The net effect of this is that on S's bank statement, the cheque will appear as having been paid in (a credit on the bank statement),and then later will appear as having been paid out (a debit on the bank statement).

The original credit on the bank statement will be in S's cash book as a debit in the normal way. But the debit on the bank statement (the dishonour of the cheque) will not be in S's cash book. This will have to be credited into the cash book as money paid out.

These cheques are technically referred to as 'returned cheques', but they are also called 'dishonoured cheques' or 'bounced cheques'.

Example 4

C sends a cheque to S in payment of an invoice for £300.

(a)   S will enter this cheque into his accounts as follows: Cash book

Cash book

	£		£
SLCA	300		

SLCA

	£		£
		Cash book	300

The cheque will appear on S's bank statement as a credit entry.

KAPLAN PUBLISHING

(b) When the cheque is dishonoured S will enter this cheque into his accounts as follows:

Cash book

	£		£
		SLCA	300

SLCA

	£		£
Cash book	300		

The journal entry will be

Dr   SLCA   300

Cr   Cash book   300

This reinstates the receivable.

The dishonoured cheque will appear on the bank statement as a debit entry.

 Test your understanding 3

Given below is the cash book of a business and the bank statement for the week ending 20 April 20X1.

Required:

Compare the cash book to the bank statement and note any differences that you find.

Cash book

		£			£
16/4	Donald & Co	225.47	16/4	Balance b/d	310.45
17/4	Harper Ltd	305.68	17/4	Cheque 03621	204.56
	Fisler Partners	104.67	18/4	Cheque 03622	150.46
18/4	Denver Ltd	279.57	19/4	Cheque 03623	100.80
19/4	Gerald Bros	310.45		Cheque 03624	158.67
20/4	Johnson & Co	97.68	20/4	Cheque 03625	224.67
			20/4	Balance c/d	173.91
		1,323.52			1,323.52

EXPRESS BANK			CONFIDENTIAL	

High Street   Account   CURRENT   Sheet no. 0213
Fenbury
TL4 6JY   Account name P L DERBY LTD
Telephone: 0169 422130
      Statement date 20 April 20X1   Account Number 40429107

Date	Details	Withdrawals (£)	Deposits (£)	Balance (£)
16/4	Balance from sheet 0212			310.45 OD
17/4	DD – District Council	183.60		494.05 OD
18/4	Credit		225.47	
19/4	Credit		104.67	
	Cheque 03621	240.56		
	Bank interest	3.64		408.11 OD
20/4	Credit		305.68	
	Credit		279.57	
	Cheque 03622	150.46		
	Cheque 03624	158.67		131.99 OD

DD	Standing order	DD	Direct debit	CP	Card purchase
AC	Automated cash	OD	Overdrawn	TR	Transfer

Test your understanding 4

Graham

The cash account of Graham showed a debit balance of £204 on 31 March 20X3. A comparison with the bank statements revealed the following:

		£
1	Cheques drawn but not presented	3,168
2	Amounts paid into the bank but not credited	723
3	Entries in the bank statements not recorded in the cash account	
	(i) Standing orders	35
	(ii) Interest on bank deposit account	18
	(iii) Bank charges	14
4	Balance on the bank statement at 31 March	2,618

Tasks

(a) Show the appropriate adjustments required in the cash account of Graham bringing down the correct balance at 31 March 20X3.

(b) Prepare a bank reconciliation statement at that date.

Test your understanding 5

The following are the cash book and bank statements of KT Ltd.

Receipts June 20X1

	CASH BOOK – JUNE 20X1			
Date	Details	Total	Sales ledger control	Other
1 June	Balance b/d	7,100.45		
8 June	Cash and cheques	3,200.25	3,200.25	–
15 June	Cash and cheques	4,100.75	4,100.75	–
23 June	Cash and cheques	2,900.30	2,900.30	–
30 June	Cash and cheques	6,910.25	6,910.25	–
		£24,212.00	£17,111.55	

Payments June 20X1

Date	Payee	Cheque no	Total £	Purchase ledger control £	Operating overhead £	Admin overhead £	Other £
1 June	Hawsker Chemical	116	6,212.00	6,212.00			
7 June	Wales Supplies	117	3,100.00	3,100.00			
15 June	Wages and salaries	118	2,500.00		1,250.00	1,250.00	
16 June	Drawings	119	1,500.00				1,500.00
18 June	Blyth Chemical	120	5,150.00	5,150.00			
25 June	Whitby Cleaning Machines	121	538.00	538.00			
28 June	York Chemicals	122	212.00	212.00			
			19,212.00	15,212.00	1,250.00	1,250.00	1,500.00

Bank statement

Crescent Bank plc			Statement no: 721	
High Street				
Sheffield			Page 1	
Account:	Alison Robb t/a KT Ltd			
Account no:	57246661			

Date	Details	Payments £	Receipts £	Balance £
20X1				
1 June	Balance b/d			8,456.45
1 June	113	115.00		8,341.45
1 June	114	591.00		7,750.45
1 June	115	650.00		7,100.45
4 June	116	6,212.00		888.45
8 June	CC		3,200.25	4,088.70
11 June	117	3,100.00		988.70
15 June	CC		4,100.75	5,089.45
15 June	118	2,500.00		2,589.45
16 June	119	1,500.00		1,089.45
23 June	120	5,150.00		4,060.55 O/D
23 June	CC		2,900.30	1,160.25 O/D

Key:	S/O	Standing Order	DD	Direct Debit
	CC	Cash and cheques	CHGS	Charges
	BACS	Bankers automated clearing	O/D	Overdrawn

Task

Examine the business cash book and the business bank statement shown in the data provided above. Prepare a bank reconciliation statement as at 30 June 20X1. Set out your reconciliation in the proforma below.

Proforma

BANK RECONCILIATION STATEMENT AS AT 30 JUNE 20X1

£

Balance per bank statement
Outstanding lodgements:

Unpresented cheques:

Balance per cash book £

4 Summary

In this chapter we have explored the concept of the bank reconciliation and produced some examples, after producing an updated cash book. Do note that when comparing the bank statement to the cash book, figures appearing on the bank statement may be from the cash book some time ago due to the nature of the clearing system.

Test your understanding answers

Test your understanding 1

	£
Opening balance	(673.42)
Payments	(6,419.37)
Receipts	6,488.20
Closing balance	(604.59)

The closing balance is £604.59 overdrawn.

Test your understanding 2

Updated cash book:

Date	Details	£	Date	Chq	Details	£
			1 May		Balance b/d	526
6 May	Shaws	630	3 May	0041	Bills Farm	2,000
6 May	Andrew Ltd	880	3 May	0042	Cows Head	3,240
10 May	BACS	6,200	5 May	0043	Adam Ant	840
25 May	Bank Interest	40	30 May	0044	Miles to Go	700
31 May	BACS	460				
			31 May		Balance c/d	904
		8,210				8,210
1 June	Balance b/d	904				

Test your understanding 3

Cash book

		£			£
16/4	Donald & Co	225.47✓	16/4	Balance b/d	310.45✓
17/4	Harper Ltd	305.68✓	17/4	Cheque 03621	204.56
	Fisler Partners	104.67✓	18/4	Cheque 03622	150.46✓
18/4	Denver Ltd	279.57✓	19/4	Cheque 03623	100.80
19/4	Gerald Bros	310.45		Cheque 03624	158.67✓
20/4	Johnson & Co	97.68	20/4	Cheque 03625	224.67
			20/4	Balance c/d	173.91
		1,323.52			1,323.52

There are three unticked items on the bank statement:

- direct debit £183.60 to the District Council

- cheque number 03621 £240.56 – this has been entered into the cash book as £204.56

- bank interest £3.64.

Cheques 03623 and 03625 are unticked items in the cash book but these are payments that have not yet cleared through the banking system. Also the receipts from Gerald Bros and Johnson & Co have not yet cleared the banking system.

EXPRESS BANK				CONFIDENTIAL	
Date	Details	Withdrawals (£)	Deposits (£)	Balance (£)	
16/4	Balance from sheet 0212			310.45 OD	
17/4	DD – District Council	183.60		494.05 OD	
18/4	Credit		225.47✓		
19/4	Credit		104.67✓		
	Cheque 03621	240.56			
	Bank interest	3.64		408.11 OD	
20/4	Credit		305.68✓		
	Credit		279.57✓		
	Cheque 03622	150.46✓			
	Cheque 03624	158.67✓		131.99 OD	
DD	Standing order	DD	Direct debit	CP	Card purchase
AC	Automated cash	OD	Overdrawn	TR	Transfer

Test your understanding 4

(a)

Cash account

	£		£
Balance b/d	204	Sundry accounts	
Interest on deposit account	18	Standing orders	35
		Bank charges	14
		Balance c/d	173
	222		222
Balance b/d	173		

(b)

BANK RECONCILIATION STATEMENT AT 31 MARCH 20X3

	£
Balance per bank statement	2,618
Add Outstanding lodgements	723
	3,341
Less Unpresented cheques	(3,168)
Balance per cash account	173

KAPLAN PUBLISHING

Test your understanding 5

BANK RECONCILIATION STATEMENT AS AT 30 JUNE 20X1

	£	£
Balance per bank statement		(1,160.25) O/D
Outstanding lodgements: 30 June		6,910.25
		5,750.00
Unpresented cheques:		
121	538.00	
122	212.00	
		(750.00)
Balance per cash book (7,100.45 + 17,111.55 – 19,212.00)		£5,000.00

The banking system

Introduction

This chapter will introduce you to the banking system and the terminology used within this system.

ASSESSMENT CRITERIA
Identify the appropriate use of different payment methods (1.1)
Identify the effect of different payment methods on the bank balance (1.2)

CONTENTS

1 Bank and customer relationship
2 Banking services
3 Banking procedures
4 The clearing system
5 Cheques
6 Transferring money by different methods
7 Credit cards and debit cards
8 Banking documentation
9 Document retention and security

1 Bank and customer relationship

1.1 Introduction

The relationship between the bank and the customer can be described best as that of a receivable and payable.

1.2 Receivable/payable relationship

This is the basic bank/customer relationship. If the bank holds money belonging to the customer, the money has to be repaid at some time, and therefore from the bank's point of view, the customer is the **payable** (i.e. the bank owes money). From the customer's point of view the bank is the receivable (i.e. the customer is owed money by the bank).

However, when the customer borrows money from the bank the relationship is reversed. For the bank the customer is the **receivable** and for the customer the bank is the **payable**.

This is the case not only if a business has a loan from the bank but also if the business has an overdraft with a bank. In this situation the business owes the bank money.

1.3 Banking terminology

The usual meanings of debit and credit in double entry bookkeeping in the context of cash are:

- debit – money into the bank account
- credit – money out of the bank account.

On a bank statement these meanings are reversed as the statement is prepared from the bank's point of view.

When a customer has money in the bank account this is described by the bank as a credit balance. If the customer has an overdraft then this is described as a debit balance.

2 Banking services

2.1 Introduction

Traditionally, there was more of a difference between the services offered by banks and those offered by building societies. However since banking laws were changed, building societies are able to offer more services that are equivalent to those offered by banks. People and businesses have bank accounts so they do not have to keep all their money as cash.

There are three main types of bank account:

- current accounts
- deposit or savings accounts
- loan accounts.

2.2 Current accounts

The current account is a business's normal working account. Cash and cheques received from customers are paid into this account and the business will be issued with a cheque book so that expenses and suppliers can be paid by writing cheques.

Current accounts are also the most common form of account for personal customers.

2.3 Overdraft

Most banks, on request, will allow a business (or indeed a personal customer) an agreed level of overdraft. This means that on occasions if the current account does not have enough funds to cover cheques written the bank will still honour those cheques up to the overdraft limit. The bank will charge interest on any overdrawn balances and often an arrangement fee for the setting up of the overdraft facility.

2.4 Deposit accounts

Deposit accounts, or savings accounts, are held by many business and personal customers. A business can use a deposit account to house short-term surplus funds as the interest earned on deposit account balances is often considerably higher than that on current account balances. Money in deposit accounts can then be transferred to the current account when required but some types of account do require a period of notice before funds can be transferred or removed from the account.

2.5 Loan accounts

Although an overdraft on a current account can be a useful method of short term borrowing in order to fund the everyday expenses of a business, if larger funds are required for example for the purchase of plant and machinery in a business, then a separate loan should be taken out.

A business loan can be made to all types of business and will normally be secured. This means that the bank will have rights over assets of the business if the loan is not repaid or alternatively the personal guarantee of the owner of the business will be required.

For the purchase of property a commercial mortgage can be provided. This is normally for a period of 25 years and is secured on the property itself. Therefore if the mortgage is not repaid, the bank can sell the property in order to get its money back.

3 Banking procedures

3.1 Getting payment for the customer

When a customer pays a cheque into their bank account which has been received from another person, the customer is asking the branch to obtain payment from the other person's bank account and credit it to (i.e. pay it into) his or her bank account.

3.2 Paying in cash and cheques

The individual who is paying in monies takes the cash, cheques and paying in book to the bank and hands them to the cashier behind the counter.

The cashier ensures that the amounts being paid in agree to the paying in slip which has been completed by the individual.

Any cash paid in will be credited direct to the business's account when the branch records all the transactions for the day.

Cheques paid in are sorted and put through the clearing system.

4 The clearing system

4.1 Introduction

The major banks have developed a system known as the clearing system which is the method by which the banks exchange cheques.

4.2 How the clearing system works

The whole process of clearing cheques takes three working days.

Day 1

The branch of the bank (the collecting bank) will have received cheques paid in by customers written by third parties who have their accounts at:

- other clearing banks
- other branches of the same bank.

At the end of the day these cheques are:

- sorted by the bank
- stamped with details of the branch/bank
- processed through a machine which puts the amount payable onto the bottom of the cheque in code.

The cheques are then sent by courier to the bank's own clearing department.

Day 2

The bank's clearing department receives cheques from all its branches. It will now:

- sort the cheques by bank
- take other banks' cheques to the Central Clearing House
- send the cheques relating to its own branches to those branches without sending them to the clearing house (this is inter-branch clearing).

The central clearing house arranges for all the banks involved to attend to 'swap' cheques and to arrange for any differences in the values of cheques swapped to be paid on the following day.

Day 3

Each branch receives the cheques written by its own customers. The branch has to check that the cheque is valid and to return any cheques that cannot be paid.

4.3 Clearing debts

The clearing process results in banks owing money to each other.

Each clearing bank maintains an account with the Bank of England. These accounts are known as **operational balances**. These balances are used to settle the debts which arise between the banks in the course of clearing.

The operation of the clearing system means that when cheques are paid into a bank account it will take three working days before they are credited to the organisation's bank account.

 Test your understanding 1

David Cater has received a cheque for £1,000 from MEL Motor Factors Limited and has paid it into his account at the Mid-West Bank. When he asks if he can draw out some cash against the cheque, he is told by the cashier that he will have to wait four days from the date that the cheque was paid in.

Explain briefly why the bank might ask David to wait before he can draw out some or all of the £1,000.

---

5 Cheques

 Definition

Cheque – An unconditional order in writing signed by the drawer, requiring a bank to pay on demand a sum certain in money to a named person or to the bearer.

5.1 Parties to a cheque

The parties involved in a cheque are:

- the drawer – the person writing the cheque.

- the payee – the person the cheque is to be paid to.

- the drawee – the bank upon whom the cheque is drawn, i.e. the bank who has issued the cheque book.

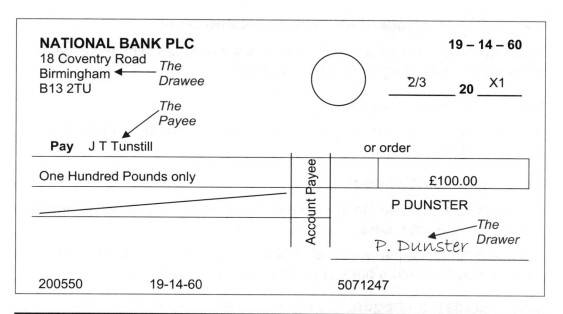

NATIONAL BANK PLC   19 – 14 – 60

18 Coventry Road
Birmingham   ◄── *The Drawee*
B13 2TU

         The Payee

         2/3   **20** X1

Pay   J T Tunstill   or order

One Hundred Pounds only   £100.00

Account Payee

P DUNSTER

P. Dunster   ◄── *The Drawer*

200550   19-14-60   5071247

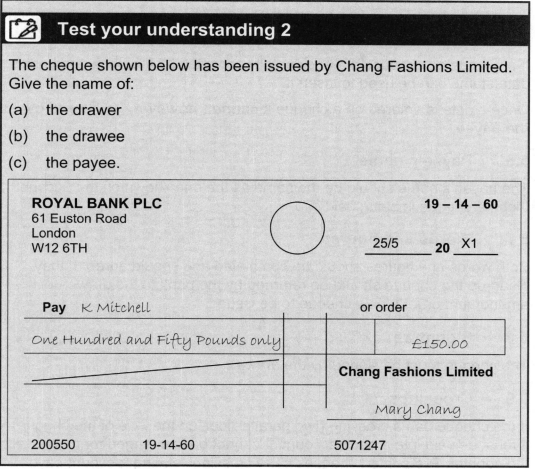

Test your understanding 2

The cheque shown below has been issued by Chang Fashions Limited. Give the name of:

(a)   the drawer

(b)   the drawee

(c)   the payee.

ROYAL BANK PLC   19 – 14 – 60

61 Euston Road
London
W12 6TH

        25/5   **20** X1

Pay   K Mitchell   or order

One Hundred and Fifty Pounds only   £150.00

Chang Fashions Limited

Mary Chang

200550   19-14-60   5071247

5.2 Checking cheques – the collecting bank

When the bank accepts a cheque which has been paid in by a customer, the bank must carefully review that cheque.

5.3 Out of date cheque

A cheque can become out of date as it is only valid for **six months** from the date of issue.

5.4 Post-dated cheque

A cheque which is dated later than the day on which it is written cannot be paid in until that later date.

For example, a cheque written on 5 May 20X1 but dated 10 May 20X1 could not be paid into a bank account before 10 May 20X1.

5.5 Undated cheque

If a cheque is presented to the payee undated the payee can insert a date. The bank's cashier would normally ask the payee to do this.

If any undated cheques are accidentally accepted by the bank, the bank's date stamp can be used to insert it.

Once a date is entered on a cheque it **cannot, however, be altered by the payee.**

5.6 Payee's name

The payee's name should be the same as the one shown on the account that the cheque is being paid into.

5.7 Words and figures

Both words and figures should be completed and should agree. If they disagree the cheque should be returned by the bank to the drawer for amendment or for a new cheque to be issued.

5.8 Signature

The cheque must be signed by the drawer.

5.9 Crossings

If the cheque has a crossing (two parallel lines on the face of the cheque), it must be paid into a bank account. It cannot be exchanged for cash over the counter. Pre-printed cheques carry crossings stating "account payee only". This means the cheque can only be paid into the account of the payee.

5.10 Stopped cheques

A customer has the right to stop a cheque right up until the banker pays it. The customer must write to the bank and give clear details of the payee's name, the cheque's number and the amount payable.

5.11 The sort code

The sort code is 6 numbers. This is a number unique to each branch of every bank. It is printed on every cheque that the particular branch issues and can be read by a computer.

 Test your understanding 3

A cheque for £374 has been accepted by one of the cashiers in payment for a washing machine. As you record the cheque, you notice that it has been dated 1 June 20X2. Today's date is 1 June 20X3.

(a) Will payment of the cheque by the drawer's bank be affected by the incorrect date?

(b) Having noticed the error, is it acceptable for you to alter the cheque to the correct date?

6 Transferring money by different methods

6.1 Introduction

A bank customer can transfer money from his account to another person's account by two other methods which do not involve the cheque clearing system or writing cheques. These are:

- standing orders
- direct debits.

6.2 Standing order

This is an instruction to a customer's bank to make regular payments (usually fixed amounts).

To arrange a standing order, all the customer needs to do is sign a **standing order mandate** which authorises the bank to make the payments.

Standing orders are ideal for paying regular monthly bills such as insurance premiums. They can also be used to transfer money between a customer's own different accounts, e.g. transferring surplus money each month from a current account into a deposit account where it will earn interest.

6.3 Standing order mandate

To **FINANCIAL BANK PLC**		

_____ Branch STANDING ORDER MANDATE

	Bank	Branch title (not address)	Sort code number
Please pay			
	Beneficiary's name		Account number
Credit			
	Amount in figures	Amount in words	
the sum of	£		
commencing	Date of first payment		Due date & frequency
	now/*	And thereafter every	
	Date and amount of last payment		
until		£	*until you receive further notice from me/us in writing
quoting the reference			and debit my/our account accordingly

Please cancel any previous standing order or direct debit in favour of the named beneficiary above

Special instructions

Account to be debited	Account number

Signature (s)

Date

_____

* Delete if not applicable

6.4 Direct debit

This is an instruction to a customer's bank to allow a third party to debit (i.e. collect money from) the customer's account at regular intervals.

Direct debits are better than standing orders when either

- the amount is uncertain or
- the date of payment is uncertain.

Direct debits are useful for paying items such as membership subscriptions which increase from year to year or monthly bills which alter in amount each month such as credit card bills.

Both direct debits and standing orders continue to be valid until the customer cancels or changes them.

Test your understanding 4

Music World Limited needs to make regular monthly payments to Firmcare Finance Limited. The amount of the payment varies from month to month. Which service provided by the banks would appear to be the most appropriate?

6.5 Electronic clearing

To try to reduce the number of pieces of paper used to clear payments using the cheque clearing and giro clearing systems, a further service was introduced in 1968.

This service is known as BACS (Bankers Automated Clearing System) and is part of the clearing system.

BACS – A method of clearing payments in which transactions are recorded on magnetic tape or disks (rather than on paper).Transactions are then processed at the BACS computer centre instead of through the clearing house.

BACS can be used by banks or by companies which have been allowed to do so by the banks.

6.6 Use of BACS

BACS is used for:

- standing order payments
- direct debits
- salary payments.

6.7 CHAPS

A further service is also available to customers wishing to transfer large sums of money. This is CHAPS (Clearing House Automated Payments System).

Payments are credited to the payee on the same day as instructions are received, so this is useful when the money needs to clear immediately.

7 Credit cards and debit cards

7.1 Credit cards

Credit cards are issued by the credit card companies to allow customers to make purchases (without using cash or cheques) at certain shops, hotels, websites, etc.

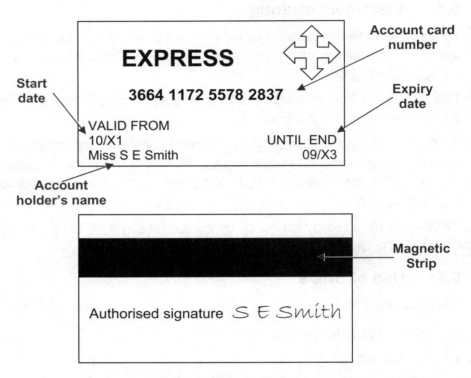

An individual opens an account with one of the credit card companies, filling in and posting off an application form. If accepted, the individual will receive a credit card.

This credit card can then be used in places which accept that particular card.

7.2   Payment of the credit card balance

Once a month, the credit cardholder receives a statement detailing how much he has 'spent' which is the amount he owes the credit card company.

The cardholder has a choice of:

- paying a minimum balance (set by the credit card company dependent upon the amount owed)

- paying off more than the minimum but less than the total balance outstanding

- paying off the total balance outstanding.

If the cardholder does not pay off the total balance within 25 days of receiving the statement, he will have to pay interest on the unpaid amount.

7.3   Accepting credit cards

Businesses which make direct sales to the public are generally known as retailers. If a retailer is to be able to accept payment by credit cards, he or she must have the agreement of the credit card company to be allowed to accept payment by that particular credit card.

In return for this service the credit card company will normally charge a commission on each payment using that card.

7.4   Debit cards

A debit card is a method of making payment direct from a bank account without having to write out a cheque. Debit cards are issued by the main banks.

When a debit card is used to make a payment the cardholder's bank account is automatically debited with the amount of the payment. The payment then appears on the customer's bank statement along with cheque payments, standing orders and direct debits.

8   Banking documentation

8.1   Bank statement

A bank statement is a statement showing how money has gone into or left a bank account, and the amount of money held in that account at a certain date. There is a standard format with a few variations between banks.

FINANCIAL BANK plc		CONFIDENTIAL

YOU CAN BANK ON US

10 Yorkshire Street   Account   CURRENT   Sheet no.   103
Headingley   MISS ELIZABETH DERBY
Leeds LS1 1QT
Telephone: 0113 633061   *Name and address*   *Name of account*
                        of bank   *holder*

Statement date 31 July 20X5   Account Number   34786695

Date	Details		Withdrawals (£)	Deposits (£)	Balance (£)
28 June	*Balance from sheet no.* **102**				2,670.91
1 July	000354		7.95		
	Security Insurance	DD	10.15		
	Leeds Brigate	AC	50.00		
	NWWA	DD	13.03		2,589.78
2 July	Supersaver	CP	12.63		2,577.15
5 July	000349		40.00		2,537.15
8 July	000348		18.80		2,518.35
11 July	Sure Building Society	DD	327.74		
	000346		29.80		
	Deposit account	TR	250.00		1,910.81
14 July	English Gas	SO	12.50		1,898.31
17 July	000355		30.95		1,867.36
20 July	English Electricity	SO	5.00		1,862.36
22 July	000356		50.00		1,812.36
25 July	000351		11.29		1,801.07
29 July	000352		5.29		
	000350		50.00		
	PAYROLL			340.99	2,086.77
30 July	000358		26.51		
	Balance to Sheet no. **104**				2,060.26

SO	Standing order	DD	Direct debit	CP	Card purchase	
AC	Automated cash	OD	Overdrawn	TR	Transfer	*Closing balance*

8.2   Paying money into the bank

Money may be paid into the bank account free of charge in any branch of that particular bank. Other banks may charge a small fee.

The money paid in can be:

- cash

- cheques

- postal orders.

The amounts to be paid in must be summarised on a paying-in slip.

    KAPLAN PUBLISHING

8.3   Paying-in slip

A paying-in slip is a summary of details of money paid into a bank account. There is a standard format with a few variations between banks.

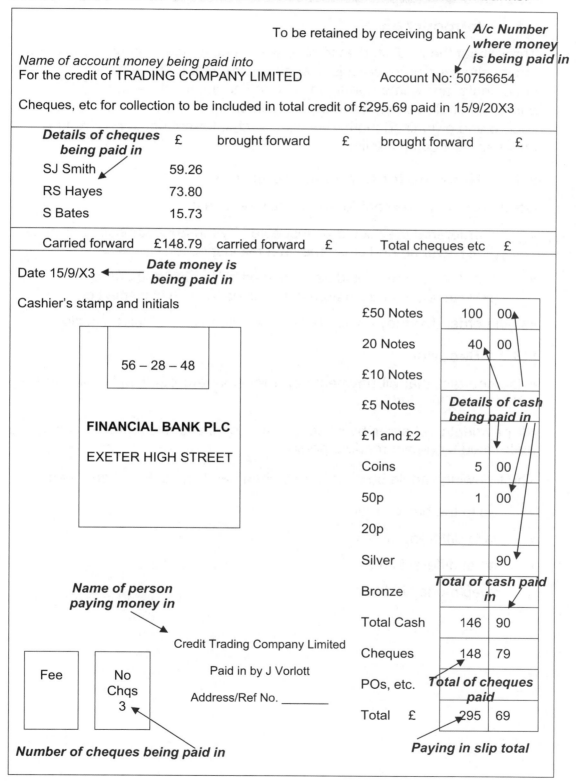

9 Document retention and security

9.1 Introduction

Throughout the AAT studies to date we will have seen many documents that businesses produce. It is a legal requirement that all financial documents, and some non-financial documents, must be kept by a business for six years. Therefore it is essential that a business has a secure and organised method of filing such information, to ensure that they can be located easily.

9.2 Reasons for document retention

Documents must be kept for three main reasons:

- in order that they could be inspected by the tax authorities (HM Revenue and Customs) in a tax inspection

- in order that they could be inspected by the tax authorities (HM Revenue and Customs) in a sales tax (VAT) inspection

- in order that they could be used as evidence in any legal action.

9.3 Security

It is important that all payments and receipts are dealt with appropriately with security in mind.

All payments, whether by cheque, cash or electronic transfer should be authorised by an appropriate person.

The following should be considered when banking cash and cheques:

- go to the bank in pairs
- take different routes
- go at different times
- keep money hidden.

Test your understanding 5

Which of the following things can NOT be determined from a customer's credit card (you can choose more than one answer).

	✓
The customer's name	
The customer's address	
The customer's credit card number	
The customer's credit limit	
The customer's credit card company	
The available amount the customer has to spend	

Test your understanding 6

Indicate whether each of the following statements is true or false.

	True/False
When a cheque is banked the funds are available immediately	
A bank cheque has to be passed to the bank of the issuer before the money becomes available	
The clearing process is quicker for a building society than for a bank	
Cheques can only be processed by banks, not building societies	
Dishonoured cheques are returned to the drawer	
The drawer has the right to stop a cheque right up until the banker pays it	

10 Summary

In this chapter you have been introduced to some of the details of the UK banking system. In particular you need to be aware of how the clearing system works, of the different methods of payment through the banking system and how credit and debit cards work. Of particular importance are the details regarding cheques, as you will need to understand what makes a valid cheque and be able to deal with a cheque that you receive that is not valid.

Test your understanding answers

Test your understanding 1

The cheque must pass through the clearing system before the Mid-West Bank knows whether or not it has been paid. In the meantime, the bank may be reluctant to allow David to draw out cash against uncleared funds.

Test your understanding 2

(a)   Mary Chang, on behalf of Chang Fashions Limited.

(b)   Royal Bank plc.

(c)   K Mitchell.

Test your understanding 3

(a)   Yes. The cheque is out of date and must be re-issued by the drawer.

(b)   No.

Test your understanding 4

Direct debit. Standing order is not appropriate since the amount of the payment varies from month to month.

Test your understanding 5

The customer's name	
The customer's address	✓
The customer's credit card number	
The customer's credit limit	✓
The customer's credit card company	
The available amount the customer has to spend	✓

Test your understanding 6

	True/False
When a cheque is banked the funds are available immediately *Explanation – Cheques need to go through a clearing process with funds normally available after 3 days*	FALSE
A bank cheque has to be passed to the bank of the issuer before the money becomes available	TRUE
The clearing process is quicker for a building society than for a bank *Explanation – The clearing process is either the same length of time or longer for building societies than for banks*	FALSE
Cheques can only be processed by banks, not building societies *Explanation – Building societies also offer banking services and so can process cheques*	FALSE
Dishonoured cheques are returned to the drawer	TRUE
The drawer has the right to stop a cheque right up until the banker pays it	TRUE

KAPLAN PUBLISHING

MOCK ASSESSMENT

1 **Mock Assessment Questions**

Task 1 **(12 marks)**

(a) Adams and Son received a cheque from a customer Polly Popper. Polly Popper banks with Le Banque Bank and Adams and Son banks with Carlton Bank plc.

(i) Who is the payee?

	✓
Adams and Son	
Polly Popper	
Carlton Bank plc	
Le Banque Bank	

(ii) Who is the drawer?

Adams and Son	
Polly Popper	
Carlton Bank plc	
Le Banque Bank	

(iii) Who is the drawee?

Adams and Son	
Polly Popper	
Carlton Bank plc	
Le Banque Bank	

(b) Show whether each of the statements below is true or false.

When Adams and Son makes payments to suppliers by credit card, the amount leaves the bank current account immediately.

True / False

When Adams and Son makes payments to suppliers by debit card, the amount paid does not affect the bank current account.

True / False

(c) Show which of the errors below are, or are not, disclosed by the trial balance.

Error in the general ledger	Error disclosed by the trial balance	Error NOT disclosed by the trial balance
Recording a bank payment for purchases on the debit side of both the bank and purchases account.		
Recording a payment for rent and rates in a non-current assets account.		
Recording a sales invoice in the sales account only.		
Incorrectly calculating the balance brought down on the rent account.		
Recording a receipt from a receivable in the bank account and the sales (subsidiary) ledger only.		
Recording payment of £1,300 in the bank account but £130 in the motor expenses account.		

Task 2 (12 marks)

Adams & Son pays employees by cheque every month and maintains a wages control account. A summary of last month's payroll transactions is shown below:

Item	£
Gross wages	18,708
Employers' NI	2,102
Employees' NI	1,782
Income tax	3,421
Trade Union fees for employee	500

Record the journal entries needed in the general ledger to:

(a) Record the wages expense.

(b) Record the HM Revenue and Customs liability.

(c) Record the net wages paid to the employees.

(d) Record the Trade Union liability.

Select your account names from the following list: Bank, Employees NI, Employers NI, HM Revenue and Customs, Income tax, Net wages, Trade Union, Wages control, Wages expense.

(a)

Account name	Amount £	Debit ✓	Credit ✓

(b)

Account name	Amount £	Debit ✓	Credit ✓

(c)

Account name	Amount £	Debit ✓	Credit ✓

(d)

Account name	Amount £	Debit ✓	Credit ✓

Task 3 (10 marks)

A credit customer, Foster's has ceased trading, owing Adams & Son £2,000 plus VAT

(a) Record the journal entries needed in the general ledger to write off Foster's debt.

Select your account names from the following list: Adams & Son, Irrecoverable debts, Foster's, Purchases, Purchases ledger control, Sales, Sales ledger control, VAT

Account name	Amount £	Debit ✓	Credit ✓

(b) Adams & Son needs help to open up some opening balances for this year's financial statements, and has given you a partially complete list of balances.

Complete the journal below by showing whether each balance would be a debit or a credit balance.

Account name	Balance (£)	Debit	Credit
Capital	8,000		
Bank overdraft	450		
Wages expense	760		
Discounts received	230		
Sales	6,430		
Bank loan	2,000		
Sales ledger control account	3,120		
Telephone expense	250		
Discounts allowed	170		
VAT payable to HMRC	600		

Task 4 (10 marks)

The following is an extract from Adam & Son's books of prime entry.

Totals for quarter

Sales day-book
Net: £156,000
VAT: £31,200
Gross: £187,200

Purchases day-book
Net: £80,000
VAT: £16,000
Gross: £96,000

Sales returns day-book
Net: £4,000
VAT: £800
Gross: £4,800

Purchases returns day-book
Net: £2,000
VAT: £400
Gross: £2,400

Cash book
Net cash sales: £1,000
VAT: £200
Gross cash sales: £1,200

(a) What will be the entries in the VAT control account to record the VAT transactions in the quarter?

Select your entries for the 'Details' columns from the following list: Cash book, Cash Sales, Purchases, Purchases returns, Purchases Sales, Sales returns, VAT.

VAT control

Details	Amount £	Details	Amount £

The VAT return has been completed and shows an amount owed to the tax authorities of £15,000.

(b) Is the VAT return correct? Yes / No

Task 5   (14 marks)

This is a summary of transactions with customers of Mini Adams during the month of June.

(a) Show whether each entry will be a debit or credit in the sales ledger control account in the general ledger.

Details	Amount £	Debit ✓	Credit ✓
Balance of receivables at 1 June	69,876		
Sales made on credit	42,090		
Receipts from credit customers	32,453		
Discounts allowed	1,459		
Goods returned by credit customers	1,901		

(b) What will be the balance brought down on 1 July on the above account?

	✓
Dr £69,876	
Cr £8,027	
Dr £76,153	
Cr £76,153	
Dr £111,534	
Cr £111,534	

The following debit balances were in the sales ledger on 1 July.

	£
Barr Ltd	23,453
Lou Lou	11,432
Grass Garden	1,200
Convent & Co	17,860
Trolls	18,080
Garvel	5,587

(c) Reconcile the balances shown above with the sales ledger control account balance you have calculated in part (b).

	£
Sales ledger control account balance as at 1 July	
Total of sales ledger accounts as at 1 July	
Difference	

It is important to reconcile the sales ledger control account on a regular basis.

(d) Which of the following statements is true?

	✓
Reconciliation of the sales ledger control account assures managers that the amount showing as outstanding from customers is correct	
Reconciliation of the sales ledger control account assures managers that the amount showing as outstanding to suppliers is correct	
Reconciliation of the sales ledger control account will show if a purchase invoice has been omitted from the sales ledger	
Reconciliation of the sales ledger control account will show if a purchase invoice has been omitted from the purchases ledger	

Task 6 (10 marks)

On 29 June Adams received the following bank statement as at 24 June.

Assume today's date is 30 June, unless told otherwise.

Carlton Bank plc

56 Armour Street, Rochdale, RO1 8YT

To: Mini Adams   Account No 82730193   24 June 20XX

Statement of account

Date	Detail	Paid out	Paid in	Balance	
20XX		£	£	£	
06 Jun	Balance b/f			12,000	C
06 Jun	Cheque 11231	2,131		9,869	C
06 Jun	Cheque 11232	123		9,746	C
07 Jun	Cheque 11233	892		8,854	C
07 Jun	Cheque 11234	2,141		6,713	C
07 Jun	Bank Giro Credit Wright Bro's		1,532	8,245	C
12 Jun	Cheque 11235	212		8,033	C
14 Jun	Direct Debit Pink Panther	531		7,502	C
20 Jun	Direct Debit Aldo Insurers	900		6,602	C
21 Jun	Bank charges	20		6,582	C
22 Jun	Overdraft fee	15		6,567	C
24 Jun	Paid in at Carlton Bank		300	6,867	C

D = Debit   C = Credit

The cash book as at 24 June is shown on the following page.

Cash book

Date 20XX	Details	Bank £	Date 20XX	Cheque number	Details	Bank £
01 June	Balance b/f	12,000	02 June	11231	Ally & Co	2,131
22 June	A Dude	300	02 June	11232	Mr Wong	123
23 June	XT Ltd	1,500	02 June	11233	Nina's Supplies	892
23 June	Maps Brothers	2,150	02 June	11234	Knobs & Bobs	2,141
			08 June	11235	PPP Ltd	212
			18 June	11236	Mama's Machines	2,350
			20 June	–	Aldo Insurers	900
			22 June	11237	George Richard's	5,000

(a)   Check the items on the bank statement against the items in the cash book.

(b)   Enter any items in the cash book as needed.

(c)   Total the cash book and clearly show the balance carried down at 24 June (closing balance) and brought down at 25 June (opening balance).

Select your entries for the 'Details' column from the following list: A Dude, Aldo Insurers, Ally & Co, Balance b/d, Balance c/d, Bank charges, Closing balance, George Richard's, Knobs & Bobs, Mama's Machines, Maps Brothers, Mr Wong, Nina's Supplies, Opening balance, Overdraft fees, Pink Panther, PPP Ltd, Wright Bro's, XT Ltd

Task 7 (14 marks)

On 28 June Oster Ltd received the following bank statement as at 23 June.

Assume today's date is 30 June unless told otherwise.

Money Bags Bank PLC
52 Oak Road, Timperley, SK10 8LR

To: Oster Ltd Account No 47013799 23 June 20XX

Statement of account

Date 20XX	Detail	Paid out £	Paid in £	Balance £	
04 June	Balance b/f			5,125	D
05 June	Cheque 104373	890		6,015	D
05 June	Cheque 104374	1,725		7,740	D
05 June	Cheque 104375	210		7,950	D
11 June	Cheque 104378	784		8,734	D
12 June	Bank Giro Credit Aintree and Co		1,250	7,484	D
13 June	Cheque 104376	1,275		8,759	D
15 June	Cheque 104377	725		9,484	D
20 June	Direct Debit MD County Council	400		9,884	D
23 June	Bank Charges	160		10,044	D
23 June	Overdraft Fee	90		10,134	D
23 June	Paid in at Money Bags Bank PLC		550	9,584	D

D = Debit C = Credit

The cash book at 23 June is shown on the next page.

Date 20XX	Details	Bank £	Date 20XX	Cheque no.	Details	Bank £
			01 June		Balance b/d	5,125
16 June	Beeston's	550	01 June	104373	Good Iron	890
19 June	Airfleet	3,025	01 June	104374	Ashworth & Co	1,725
22 June	Jones'	2,775	01 June	104375	Ironfit	210
12 June	Aintree	1,250	05 June	104376	OSS Ltd	1,275
			07 June	104377	Perfect Tools	725
			08 June	104378	Campden Ltd	784
			14 June	104379	Thornley	675
			14 June	104380	Castle	178
			20 June		MD Council	400
			23 June		Bank Charges	160
23 June	Balance c/d	4,637	23 June		Overdraft Fee	90
		12,237				12,237
			24 June		Balance b/d	4,637

Identify the FOUR transactions that are included in the cash book but missing from the bank statement, and complete the bank reconciliation.

Details	£	£
Balance per bank statement		
Add:		
Total to add		
Less:		
Total to subtract		
Balance as per cash book		

Select your entries for the 'Details' column from: Bank charges, Airfleet, Castle, Camden Ltd, Beestons, Jones', Thornley, MD Council, Good Iron.

Task 8 (14 marks)

Adams & Son's trial balance was extracted and did not balance. The debit column of the trial balance totalled £329,484 and the credit column totalled £329,134.

(a) What entry would be made in the suspense account to balance the trial balance?

Account name	Amount £	Debit ✓	Credit ✓
Suspense			

(b) The error has been traced to the sales returns day-book shown below.

Sales returns day-book

Date 20XX	Details	Credit note number	Total £	VAT £	Net £
31 July	Sloan's	231	2,400	400	2,000
31 July	Charlton & Bros	232	480	80	400
31 July	Matthew Manufacturers	233	1,200	200	1,000
	Totals		3,730	680	3,400

Identify the error and record the journal entries needed in the general ledger to:

(i) Remove the incorrect entry.

(ii) Record the correct entry.

(iii) Remove the suspense account balance.

Select your account names from the following list: Charlton & Bros, Matthew Manufacturers, Purchases, Purchases day-book, Purchases ledger control, Purchases returns, Purchases returns day-book, Sales, Sales day-book, Sales ledger control, Sales returns, Sales returns day-book, Sloan's, Suspense, VAT

Task 9   (10 marks)

When preparing the trial balance for Mini Adams, a suspense balance of £3,000 credit existed. All the bookkeeping errors have now been traced and the journal entries shown below have been recorded.

Journal entries

Account name	Debit £	Credit £
Heat and light	1,200	
Suspense		1,200
Suspense	4,200	
Rent and rates		4,200
Motor expenses	1,750	
Motor vehicles		1,750

Post the journal entries to the general ledger accounts. Dates are not required.

Select your entries for the 'Details' column from the following list: Balance b/d, Heat and light, Motor expenses, Motor vehicles, Rent and rates, Suspense.

Heat and light

Details	Amount £	Details	Amount £

Rent and rates

Details	Amount £	Details	Amount £

Suspense

Details	Amount £	Details	Amount £
		Balance b/d	3,000

Motor expenses

Details	Amount £	Details	Amount £

Motor vehicles

Details	Amount £	Details	Amount £

Task 10 (14 marks)

On 31 October, Adams & Son extracted an initial trial balance which did not balance, and a suspense account was opened. On 1 November journal entries were prepared to correct the errors that had been found, and clear the suspense account. The list of balances in the initial trial balance, and the journal entries to correct the errors, are shown below.

Re-draft the trial balance by placing the figures in the debit or credit column. You should take into account the journal entries which will clear the suspense account.

	Balances extracted on 31 October £	Balances at 1 November	
		Debit £	Credit £
Motor vehicles	47,284		
Fixtures and fittings	20,134		
Inventory	8,000		
Bank overdraft	1,231		
Petty cash	200		
Sales ledger control	105,872		
Purchases ledger control	67,980		
VAT owing to tax authorities	2,300		
Capital	50,000		
Sales	309,231		
Purchases	135,983		
Purchases returns	3,480		
Wages	60,131		
Motor expenses	2,312		
Office expenses	983		
Rent and rates	2,540		
Heat and light	3,214		
Insurance	2,100		
Miscellaneous expenses	1,781		
Suspense account (debit balance)	43,688		
Totals			

Journal entries

Account name	Debit £	Credit £
Sales	21,158	
Suspense		21,158
Sales	21,158	
Suspense		21,158

Account name	Debit £	Credit £
Rent and rates	686	
Suspense		686
Rent and rates	686	
Suspense		686

2 Mock Assessment Answers

Task 1

(a) (i) Payee is Adams and Son

(ii) Drawer is Polly Popper

(iii) Drawee is Le Banque Bank

(b) Show whether each of the statements below is true or false.

When Adams and Son makes payments to suppliers by credit card, the amount leaves the bank current account immediately.

False

When Adams and Son makes payments to suppliers by debit card, the amount paid does not affect the bank current account.

False

(c)

Error in the general ledger	Error disclosed by the trial balance	Error NOT disclosed by the trial balance
Recording a bank payment for purchases on the debit side of both the bank and purchases account.	✓	
Recording a payment for rent and rates in a non-current assets account.		✓
Recording a sales invoice in the sales account only.	✓	
Incorrectly calculating the balance brought down on the rent account.	✓	
Recording a receipt from a receivable in the bank account and the sales (subsidiary) ledger only.	✓	
Recording payment of £1,300 in the bank account but £130 in the motor expenses account.	✓	

Task 2

(a)

Account name	Amount £	Debit ✓	Credit ✓
Wages expense	20,810	✓	
Wages control	20,810		✓

(b)

Account name	Amount £	Debit ✓	Credit ✓
HM Revenue and Customs	7,305		✓
Wages control	7,305	✓	

(c)

Account name	Amount £	Debit ✓	Credit ✓
Bank	13,005		✓
Wages control	13,005	✓	

(d)

Account name	Amount £	Debit ✓	Credit ✓
Trade Union	500		✓
Wages control	500	✓	

Task 3

(a)

Account name	Amount £	Debit ✓	Credit ✓
Irrecoverable debts	2,000	✓	
VAT	400	✓	
Sales ledger control	2,400		✓

(b)

Account name	Balance (£)	Debit	Credit
Capital	8,000		✓
Bank overdraft	450		✓
Wages expense	760	✓	
Discounts received	230		✓
Sales	6,430		✓
Bank loan	2,000		✓
Sales ledger control account	3,120	✓	
Telephone expense	250	✓	
Discounts allowed	170	✓	
VAT payable to HMRC	600		✓

Task 4

(a)

VAT control

Details	Amount £	Details	Amount £
Sales returns (SRDB)	800	Sales (SDB)	31,200
Purchases (PDB)	16,000	Cash sales (CB)	200
		Purchases returns (PRDB)	400
Balance c/d	15,000		
	31,800		31,800
		Balance b/d	15,000

(b)   Yes

Task 5

(a)

Details	Amount £	Debit ✓	Credit ✓
Balance of receivables at 1 June	69,876	✓	
Sales made on credit	42,090	✓	
Receipts from credit customers	32,453		✓
Discounts allowed	1,459		✓
Goods returned by credit customers	1,901		✓

(b)

Dr £76,153	✓

(c)

	£
Sales ledger control account balance as at 1 July	76,153
Total of sales ledger accounts as at 1 July	77,612
Difference	1,459

(d)

Reconciliation of the sales ledger control account assures managers that the amount showing as outstanding from customers is correct	✓

Task 6

Date 20XX	Details	Bank £	Date 20XX	Cheque number	Details	Bank £
01 June	Balance b/f	12,000	02 June	11231	Ally & Co	2,131
22 June	A Dude	300	02 June	11232	Mr Wong	123
23 June	XT Ltd	1,500	02 June	11233	Nina's Supplies	892
23 June	Maps Brothers	2,150	02 June	11234	Knobs & Bobs	2,141
07 June	Wright Bro's	1,532	08 June	11235	PPP Ltd	212
			18 June	11236	Mama's Machines	2,350
			20 June	–	Aldo Insurers	900
			22 June	11237	George Richard's	5,000
			14 June		Pink Panther	531
			21 June		Bank charges	20
			22 June		Overdraft fee	15
			24 June		Balance c/d	3,167
		17,482				**17,482**
25 June	Balance b/d	3,167				

Task 7

	£	£
Balance per bank statement		−9,584
Add:		
Name: Airfleet	3,025	
Name: Jones'	2,775	
Total to add		5,800
Less:		
Name: Thornley	675	
Name: Castle	178	
Total to subtract		853
Balance as per cash book		−4,637

Task 8

(a)

Account name	Amount £	Debit ✓	Credit ✓
Suspense	350		✓

(b)   (i)

Account name	Amount £	Debit ✓	Credit ✓
SLCA	3,730	✓	

(ii)

Account name	Amount £	Debit ✓	Credit ✓
SLCA	4,080		✓

(iii)

Account name	Amount £	Debit ✓	Credit ✓
Suspense	350	✓	

Task 9

Heat and light

Details	Amount £	Details	Amount £
Suspense	1,200		

Rent and rates

Details	Amount £	Details	Amount £
		Suspense	4,200

Suspense

Details	Amount £	Details	Amount £
Rent and rates	4,200	Balance b/f	3,000
		Heat and light	1,200

Motor expenses

Details	Amount £	Details	Amount £
Motor vehicles	1,750		

Motor vehicles

Details	Amount £	Details	Amount £
		Motor expenses	1,750

Task 10

	Balances extracted on 31 October £	Balances at 1 November	
		Debit £	Credit £
Motor vehicles	47,284	47,284	
Fixtures and fittings	20,134	20,134	
Inventory	8,000	8,000	
Bank overdraft	1,231		1,231
Petty cash	200	200	
Sales ledger control	105,872	105,872	
Purchases ledger control	67,980		67,980
VAT owing to tax authorities	2,300		2,300
Capital	50,000		50,000
Sales (journal entry adjustment)	309,231		266,915
Purchases	135,983	135,983	
Purchases returns	3,480		3,480
Wages	60,131	60,131	
Motor expenses	2,312	2,312	
Office expenses	983	983	
Rent and rates (journal entry adjustment)	2,540	3,912	
Heat and light	3,214	3,214	
Insurance	2,100	2,100	
Miscellaneous expenses	1,781	1,781	
Suspense account (debit balance) (cleared)	43,688	–	–
Totals		391,906	391,906

INDEX